FINDING KARAKHAMUN
REVISED AND EXPANDED EDITION

THE COLLABORATIVE REDISCOVERY OF A LOST TOMB

By Anthony T. Browder

Finding Karakhamun
The Collaborative Rediscovery of a Lost Tomb

By Anthony T. Browder

Published by IKG
P.O. Box 73025
Washington, D.C. 20056
(301) 853-2465
www.ikg-info.com

Layout and Design:
Tony Browder, M'Bwebe Ishangi, and Free BenJamin

Photography:
Tony Browder, Tor Moore, Lance Chambers, Katherine Blakeney, Michael A. Brown, and Kweli Zakari

ISBN# 0-924944-16-1

2nd Printing
October, 2024

Printing: BCP Digital - Baltimore, MD • www.bcpdigital.com

Table of Contents

At the far end of the Dongola Reach, as the Nile bends and swings upward, streaming north toward the Fourth Cataract, it flows through the province of Napata where, in the town of Kurru and of Nuri, lie the ancient graves of kings.

These are the graves of the forgotten kings of Kush, the Black Valhalla through whose ghostly fields may still be heard the distant din of wars, the clash of Nubian and Libyan, of Nubian and Assyrian, over the ailing body of Egypt. Here lay, in their trappings of silver and bronze, the mummified horses of Piankhy, Shabaka, Shebitku and Taharka. Here lay the Black princes of the Twenty Fifth dynasty who, from circa 751 to 654 BCE., threw their shadow across the length and breadth of the Egyptian empire, almost a quarter of the African continent. They were among the last of the great sun kings of the ancient world. These kings formed the last bastion of Egyptian civilization against the advance of the alien.

Ivan Van Sertima
They Came Before Columbus

This work is lovingly dedicated to

Ankh Mi Ra

Asa G. Hilliard, III

Abu El Naga Gabriel

Ivan Van Sertima

Patricia Newton

Runoko Rashidi

Six wise, kind and generous souls,
who now know more than we, the living.

The Rosetta Stone

Foreword

The ASA Restoration Project:
Reclamation of the 25TH dynasty

The decipherment of the Rosetta Stone by Jean-François Champollion in 1822 opened up a new and revolutionary era of scholarship as applied to the recovery and re-discovery of Nile Valley civilization. Within 60 years, William Flinders Petrie had developed the systematic methods of archaeological excavation that inaugurated modern Egyptology. At critical intervals since then new research, excavation, and investigation has pushed Egyptology forward and transformed the discipline.

In recent decades it has become ever clearer that what is thought of as the civilization of Egypt—or more correctly, Kemet—is more properly and comprehensively thought of as Nile Valley civilization, encompassing Kemet and its southern neighbor, Kush (Nubio-Kush). Discoveries at Nubian Qustul of the pre-unification pharaonic kingdom of Ta-Seti plus continuing work at the pre-dynastic archaeoastronomical site of Nabta Playa, southwest of the First Cataract, are demonstrating ever more clearly that the genesis of the civilization of Kemet can only be sought in the south. Diodorus reported the fact in 40 BCE. in his Library of History and we find that at crucial moments the history of pharaonic Kemet was dynamically impacted by currents emanating from Nubio-Kush.

The pharaonic founder of the Middle Kingdom Amenemhet I was reported in the annals to have come "out of the South," the son of a woman from Ta-Seti (Nubia), to restore order and found the 12th dynasty, one of Kemet's greatest. Piankhy and his successors of the 25th dynasty in effect accomplished the same, inaugurating perhaps the last era of cultural efflorescence in dynastic Kemet. It was an era that revered and revived interest in the Old Kingdom of which the "Memphite Theology" of the Shabaka Stone is only one testimony. In Kemet, the Kushite pharaohs of the 25th dynasty were considered the legitimate line, especially since their purpose was to restore order in an increasingly chaotic political environment and re-establish the ascendancy of Amun in the religious affairs of the country. The 25th dynasty did much to rehabilitate Kemet but is perhaps the least studied of all the dynasties after the New Kingdom.

The careful and comprehensive excavation of the tomb of the Kushite nobleman Karakhamun on the West Bank of Luxor under the direction of Dr. Elena Pischikova, ably assisted by Mr. Anthony Browder, is another of those events that opens up a new door to the dynamic history of ancient Kemet, amplifying our awareness of its scope and millennia-old relationship with Kush. The 25th dynasty systematically attempted to re-connect the country to its most ancient roots in the Old Kingdom to solidify the foundation created in the remote past while providing a bedrock platform for meeting an evolving future. In the end, this mission could not be completed but in studying the 25th dynasty through excavation of the tomb of Karakhamun and others like it, it is possible to appreciate more fully the indelible bonds between Kemet and Kush stretching back to the unification of the country under Menes and therefore understand with ever greater authenticity the truest dimensions of Nile Valley civilization.

As already mentioned, the two most important movers and shakers facilitating the excavation of Karakhamun's tomb are Dr. Elena Pischikova and Mr. Anthony Browder. The story of how their collaboration was first inaugurated and developed in a manner that enables the excavation of a heretofore neglected 25th dynasty site is an inspiring story in and of itself. It is not too much to say that, through their work, they and their team will leave a permanent imprint on the present and future study of Nile Valley civilization.

Charles S. Finch, III
Atlanta, Georgia

There is no such things as the past or the future
For they all three are simultaneos.

Kashta —
King of Kush

*An event does not end at the end of its occurrence;
it continues to move, down through the ages,
influencing generation after generation.*

*Amos Wilson —
Psychologist*

Introduction

Writing **Finding Karakhamun** affords me the opportunity to share my research, analysis and interpretation of Nile Valley civilization, a field of study that has profoundly shaped my life for over four decades. It has been an inspiring journey of discovery that I am just beginning to realize has prepared me for the work that I have been engaged in over the past fifteen years and am presenting in this publication.

When I made my first trip to Egypt forty-four years ago, I had no idea I would return over sixty more times, or that I would raise funds and participate in the excavation and restoration of an Egyptian tomb. While involved in this endeavor, I not only helped reconstruct the life of a 25th dynasty Kushite priest, I also gained a greater appreciation for life, and a better understanding of death. This has been an important lesson for me as I struggled to come to terms with the passing of family and friends, and my own mortality.

What I know is that the past is prologue, and a thorough study and understanding of past events helps us better prepare for today and tomorrow. To facilitate your understanding and appreciation of **Finding Karakhamun**, I revised the original publication to include all the activities of the ASA Restoration Project in Egypt between 2008 and 2023. These activities are presented in four distinct parts within this book:

Part One is a description of the excavation project and provides an overview of the historical dynamics that shaped the lives of the people buried in the tombs of South Asasif. It provides technical information that facilitates your appreciation of the project.

Part Two is a narrative of the collaboration between Dr. Elena Pischikova, the discoverer of the tombs, and me. It details the creation of the ASA Restoration Project and the ongoing efforts to preserve the legacy of Dr. Asa Hilliard, III.

Part Three highlights important discoveries made during various excavation seasons, and

Part Four helps the reader appreciate the importance of this work, how it shapes our understanding of the past and informs our capacity to envision a future of our own design by utilizing Ancestral Intelligence.

As stated previously, working in the tomb of Karakhamun taught me a great deal about life, death – and life after life. I have come to understand what our Kushite and Kemetic ancestors understood thousands of years ago. They understood that there is no death. They knew that as long as the living remembered their Ancestors and called their names while pouring libations and bringing offerings, their Ancestors would come and continue to inspire, guide and protect them.

Tombs were built on the West Bank of the Nile because the West is the abode of the Ancestors. The living entered a tomb from the East and the spirit of the Ancestor buried in a tomb accessed their sanctuary through a Spirit Door in the West. Priests and family members conducted rituals required to call their Ancestors forth by day. Tombs were the hallowed ground where the living and the Ancestors met. The design, construction, and maintenance of this sacred environment is one of the best examples we have of Ancestral Intelligence – the means by which the living ensured their Ancestors would be remembered and thus, would live for eternity.

Finding Karakhamun is a personal account of the first Egyptian excavation funded by African Americans. As you read the narrative and look at the incredible photographs, I would like you to consider the importance of documenting primary research and sharing that knowledge with a wider community. I have invested forty-seven years researching Nile Valley history and I have found that who we were shapes who we are, and, most importantly, who we can become.

It's been said that the most important days in a person's life are: The day they were born, and the day they realize why they were born. While engaging in this excavation I have come to realize that I was born to find Karakhamun and oversee the restoration of his tomb.

As you read ***Finding Karakhamun*** and study how he honored his Ancestors, and how his descendants honored him, I trust you will be inspired to find the best in yourself and model the appropriate behavior for your descendants.

Anthony T. Browder
September 13, 2024
Washington, D.C.

Part One
The South Asasif Conservation Project

The Excavations of South Asasif

In 2006 the American–Egyptian archaeological team, headed by Dr. Elena Pischikova and working under the auspices of the Ministry of Antiquities of Egypt, started working in a group of 25th dynasty (Kushite) tombs in the South Asasif necropolis located south of Sheikh Abd el-Qurna on the Theban West Bank of Luxor, Egypt. South Asasif is located along the southern ridge of the Asasif Mountains, between the Valley of the Kings to the north and the Valley of the Queens to the south. It is south of Asasif (Dier el-Bahari) where the mortuary temple of

Elena Pischikova

Hatshepsut was built in the 18th dynasty, and directly across the road from the Ramessum, which was built in the 19th dynasty.

In order to put this ancient necropolis back on the map, the tombs of South Asasif had to be re-discovered and re-explored, as they had been practically lost since the beginning of the 20th century. The value of South Asasif to the history of private tomb decoration can hardly be overestimated since it contains the tombs of the Mayor of Waset, Fourth Priest of Amun, Karabasken (TT 391), and the First *aq* Priest of Amun (at Karnak Temple), Karakhamun (TT 223). Built during the reigns of Shabaka and Shebitku, they are the earliest known decorated Kushite tombs in an area now referred to as the Theban necropolis.

Thebes is the Greek name for the Ancient Egyptian capital *Waset*, which is currently known by its Arabic name *Luxor*. In order to fully appreciate the importance of the discoveries of South Asasif it helps to understand the relationship between Kush and Kemet—how that relationship evolved and how it has been interpreted over the centuries.

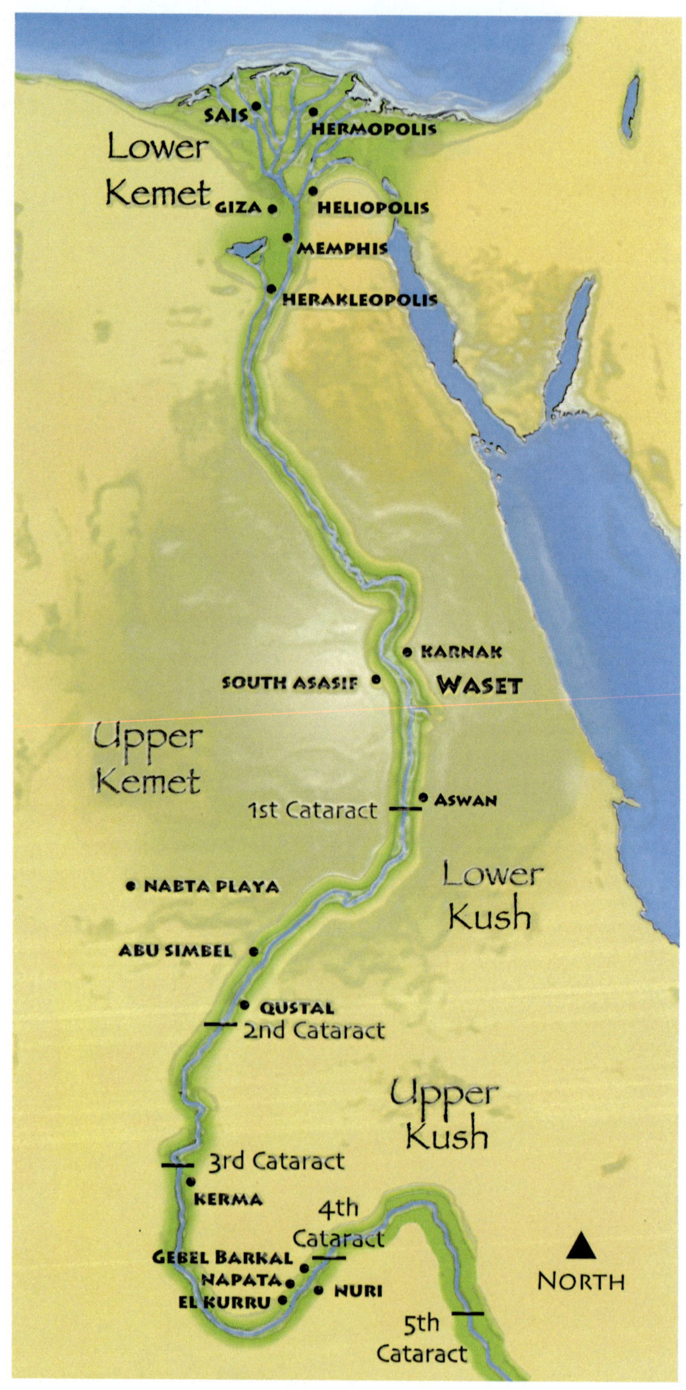

Lower Nile Valley

The Kushite 25th Dynasty and the Kingdom of Napata 713-664 BCE.

Little is known about Kush during the time between the end of the Ramesside Period and the beginning of the 25th dynasty when Kushite rulers took over Kemetic royal authority at the end of the 8th century BCE. Archaeological evidence is very scarce. The only hope to reconstruct some of the missing information is to continue the ongoing archaeological research in Egypt and undertake new projects in Sudan which focus on the early 25th dynasty monuments in Kemet and Kush. The gap between archaeological and historical information lasted from 1150 BCE until about 860 BCE.

Burials of an enigmatic ruling family, based in the town of Napata and dated to the 9th – 8th century BCE., were found in the sacred area of the cliff of Gebel Barkal and El-Kurru cemetery in Kush. The tombs of El-Kurru are mostly uninscribed and almost completely plundered, yet even the fragments of a few found objects show the tradition of an ancient elaborate funerary cult. These are the graves of the ancestors of the kings who ruled Kemet in the 25th dynasty.

The first local ruler whose name is known to us is Alara (780-760 BCE.). It is unclear if he had any cultural contacts with Kemet, but it seems he was a passionate follower of the cult of Amun. His brother Kashta (760-747 BCE.) proclaimed himself the king of Upper and Lower Kemet. Although there is no evidence left of a military campaign, Kashta is known to have visited Kemet to receive the divine mandate to rule in the name of Amun.

The first of the Napatan kings known to have conquered Kemet was Piankhy (747-713 BCE.), the son of Kashta. Piankhy reached Waset (in Upper Kemet), where he participated in various temple rituals paying respect to Amun of Karnak. During his campaign he invaded the city of Memphis (in Lower Kemet) and received submission from the local rulers. Piankhy allowed the defeated leaders to retain governorships in the northern cities of Sais, Hermopolis and Herakleopolis. He did not see himself as a conqueror of Kemet but as a protector of the ancient god Amun and his followers.

Piankhy did not stay in Kemet after this successful campaign and soon returned to Napata. Back at home Piankhy rebuilt the temple of

Piankhy's pyramid at El-Kurru

Amun at Gebel Barkal, which became the most important religious center of Kush. His burial at El-Kurru was the first true pyramid in the necropolis. Although completely ruined and plundered, it still retained a vast collection of Kemetic amulets and funerary objects.

The real Kushite presence in Kemet during the 25th dynasty begins with Piankhy's younger brother, Shabaka (713-698 BCE.) and Piankhy's son Shebitku (707 co-regency, 698-690 BCE. single rule). Shabaka returned to Kemet to reassert control over the country. The dynamic new Kushite rulers faced little internal opposition. Both Shabaka and his nephew became the first Kushite rulers who lived in Kemet. Shabaka established his residence in the traditional royal capital of Memphis. At the same, time control over Waset was secured by appointing Kashta's daughter Amenirdis I as the adopted daughter of the God's Wife of Amun.

The Kushite rulers of Kemet considered themselves legitimate pharaohs in the ancient tradition. Seeing their mission in Kemet as restoring what they considered the proper ancient religious order, the Kushite kings associated themselves with the great pharaohs of the past. They chose names of Fifth and Sixth dynasty pharaohs and undertook extensive renovations and renewals of ancient temples. They attempted to revive, and at times to reinvent, ancient myths, rituals, traditions, artistic styles, language, and literature. Works in all media reflect progressive archaizing tendencies.

Although well established in Kemet, all the Kushite rulers of the 25th dynasty were buried in their native land in the royal necropolae at El-Kurru and Nuri not far from the sacred site of Gebel Barkal. Kushite rulers continuously modeled their kingship and religious practices on Kemetic traditions of the past. Following Piankhy's example, Shabaka, Shebitku, and Tanutamun were buried in the now badly ruined pyramids at El-Kurru. The burials of Shabaka and Tanutamun contained a large collection of ivory plaques carved in raised relief. The exquisite quality of the carving and iconography of the offering scenes recalls the decoration of the funerary monuments of the Old Kingdom of Kemet.

Shabaka, who ruled Kemet for fifteen years, inaugurated the new Kushite phase of royal building activity. Objects and stelae inscribed for Shabaka are found in nearly every important religious center from the Delta in Kemet to his native Napata. As a builder he focused on renovating and repairing projects in many important religious centers in Kemet including the great temples of Karnak, Luxor, and Medinet Habu.

The "Shabaka stone" is another attempt to re-connect with the Kemetic past. The date of the original document remains undetermined. It could be a copy made from an old papyrus as stated on the stela or an imitation of an ancient document. At the same time Shabaka ruled Kemet, he maintained his connections with the land of his ancestors in Kush.

Unfortunately, not many images of Shabaka in sculpture and relief are known and little remains of the sculpture and relief of this period in Kemet. Besides natural causes of destruction, a large body of Kushite art was usurped and reused during the Saite Period. For example, Kushite ram's head, royal amulets and double cobras on headdresses were deliberately chiseled off and replaced by different fetishes and regalia during the 26th dynasty (664-525 BCE).

In 707, Shebitku (707-690 BCE) succeeded his uncle, Shabaka, as pharaoh. Shebitku was able to retain his substantial empire and continued building projects in Memphis and Waset. Not many representations of Shebitku survive apart from a few known images carved for Karnak temple.

After the death of Shebitku, his brother Taharka (690-664 BCE) became pharaoh. His twenty-six-year reign was the lengthiest and most prosperous of all the Kushite rulers.

Taharka's ambitious building projects included founding new temples, as well as renovating and restoring important temples of the past. Many older temples in Kemet received new additions or conservation attention under Taharka. He was as active in Kush as he was in Kemet. Impressive temple remains and numerous works of art associated with Taharka were found at many Kushite sites.

Taharka founded a new cemetery at Nuri that was used continuously by nineteen of his successors. The pyramids were built of blocks of local red sandstone and are of good masonry construction. The pyramid of Taharka, the biggest of all, may have reached 131-164 feet in height.

It's important to note that there were more pyramids built in Kush (400+) than Kemet (118). Kushite pyramids are similar in size to the smaller pyramids built in Saqqara during the 5th and 6th dynasties. They were constructed with a much steeper angle than Kemetic pyramids and had a small temple/chapel entrance. Practically every Kushite pyramid was destroyed by European tomb robbers during the early 19th century.

Taharka

Numerous statues and relief representations statues of Taharka remain in both Kemet and Nubia. Recent excavations at Kerma (Sudan) have revealed a new group of monumental statues of Taharka.

Artistically, Kushite rule was a period of great innovation. The Kushite dynasty established its own style of relief and sculpture that influenced Kemetic art until the end of the pharaonic period (30 BCE.). An important aspect of this artistic renewal was the continuation of a tradition of systematic references to the art of the past, a phenomenon often called *archaism*. Archaism in the 8th – 7th century BCE. reveals itself in many ways—from the revival of ancient forms and types of scenes and canons of proportions, to the copying of small details from older monuments. Inspired by these monuments, the sculptors were reinterpreting earlier sources while refining their own precise elegant style. Old Kingdom art was one of the main sources of inspiration for the Kushites, and the love and respect for their ancestral traditions can best be found in the tombs of South Asasif.

Through the combined efforts of the South Asasif Conservation Project and the ASA Restoration Project we have committed our time and resources to the excavation, conservation and restoration of the tombs of Karabasken, Karakhamun and Nesbanebdjed. As we learned more about the 25th dynasty, and the Kushite presence in Kemet, it became apparent that they were custodians and restorers of ancient traditions, not conquers. It is our desire that the dissemination of our work leads to a greater understanding and appreciation of the 25th dynasty in Kemet.

The Tomb of Karabasken

Karabasken, was an architect and the Mayor of Waset (the city now known as Luxor) and Fourth Priest of Amun. He was the first Kushite official to build his tomb in what is now referred to as the Theban necropolis. Thebes is the ancient Greek name for the West Bank of Waset. Karabasken was one of the highest officials in Waset during the 25th dynasty and he may have been a member of the royal family. Because of his position as mayor (and skill as an architect), Karabasken likely supervised the building projects of King Shabaka at the temples of Karnak, Luxor and Medinet Habu.

Since the time of Karabasken's glory, his tomb was damaged by floods, fire, and the locals who lived in it for long periods of time. Walls and pillars were covered in soot because of the numerous fires set for cooking and warmth. The decoration at the entrance of the tomb was chiseled off. Although the outlines of the tomb's main architectural elements were still visible, the total lack of decoration on any discernible surface offered scant hope of any meaningful reconstruction. It was considered completely lost and ruined.

Despite all these negative factors, Dr. Pischikova started clearing the tomb of Karabasken in 2006 and made a major discovery. It emerged with the removal of a six and a half feet thick debris layer and a modern mud brick structure in the deep vaulted recess in the west wall of the court. When the workers exposed the lower part of the doorframe, they saw two relatively well-preserved seated images of Karabasken with his name and titles written above him.

Karabasken is shown in the attire and style of the Old Kingdom, at least two millennia earlier. He is seated on a lion-legged chair, its short back decorated with a papyrus umbel. He wears a short, pleated kilt and a priest's pelt vest held by a sash tied on his shoulder with a large, elaborate knot, and a double amulet. This amulet consists of two overlapping drop-shaped elements on a long cord. This style of amulet became very popular during the Kushite and Saite Periods, and it appears that Karabasken is the earliest Kushite tomb owner shown with it.

Karabasken's tomb was unfinished and undecorated which suggests that he died while his tomb was being constructed, and, according to long held traditions in Kemet and Kush, the deceased must be embalmed and buried seventy days after their death.

By the late 20th century, Karabasken's tomb had been usurped by the chief of the village of Qurna who claimed it as his personal property. He used a portion of the tomb to keep his livestock and converted another area of the tomb into a family bedroom for use during hot summer nights. The ceiling of the tomb was covered with soot from the torches and fires that occupants used for light and cooking while living inside the tomb.

We used Karabasken's tomb to store fragments found while excavating the tomb of Karakhamun. The tombs are close by and storing artifacts on site makes restoration easier. We stored over 34,000 artifacts that were used to restore the tomb of Karakhamun.

The eight limestone pillars in the tomb had been badly damaged because the tomb was used as a quarry to provide building material for the construction of other homes in the village. Each pillar had gaping holes in them, which compromised their structural integrity and could have led to the imminent collapse of the ceiling had they not been restored during excavation.

Karabasken's Pillard Hall with Karakhamun fragments on floor

The tomb had also been badly damaged by flood debris and the floor was covered with four feet of compacted sand, rocks and dirt that accumulated after centuries of flash floods. Our team worked in this tomb for over a decade before we began excavating and removing the flood debris. We made several unexpected discoveries during our excavation.

Canopic jars

In 2016 we unearthed steps near the southern wall between two pillars. The steps led to a small room, and in the corner of that room was a six-foot-deep shaft that led to two burial chambers, at opposite ends of a narrow corridor. Of course, both burial chambers were empty, but as we removed the flood debris in one room, we discovered a two foot, by two foot, by two foot hole dug into the limestone floor. Inside of the hole was a complete set of canopic jars, made of the finest alabaster. One of the canopic jars was inscribed with the phrase, "Lady of the House Amenirdis." This was a title given to the daughters of Kushite kings who were referred to as the "God's Wife of Amun." This special group of priestesses were earthly representatives of Mut (the wife of Amun). They occupied a special temple on the West Bank of Waset where they conducted weekly rituals which were considered the most sacred activities during the 25th dynasty.

As we continued our excavations at the western end of Karabasken's tomb we expected to find a shaft that would lead to his burial chamber. Instead, we unearthed a twenty-six-foot-long ramp

that led to his burial compartment. Inside the confines of a narrow room, we discovered a 20,000-pound, red granite sarcophagus that measured eight feet high, five feet wide and twelve feet in length. There were no inscriptions on the sarcophagus and the body it once contained disappeared ages ago. But the discovery of the sarcophagus provided us with two crucial pieces of information about its former occupant.

1. Red granite is a stone reserved for royalty.
2. The royal quarry for red granite was in Aswan which is 133miles south of Waset.

While we found scant information about the life of Karabasken, it was safe to assume that he was an important figure to have such a large private tomb and to have been buried in a sarcophagus fit for royalty. Because Karabasken's tomb was devoid of inscriptions and there were no traces of a body, jewelry or funerary equipment found in his burial chamber we were left with more questions than answers. We have no idea when the burial chamber was robbed. It could have been desecrated by members of the 26th dynasty, who had also usurped the tombs of Karakhamun and Nesbanebdjed. It could have been robbed by the Greeks or Romans when they occupied ancient Thebes, or it could have been robbed by any number of people, any number of times over the last 27 centuries.

These questions may never be answered, but at least for the present I'm grateful that our team was there to excavate these tombs, restore them to their former glory and honor the memory of the Kushite nobles for whom they were built.

Ramp burial compartment and sarcophagus of Karabasken

Karabasken's 1st Pillared Hall – 2006

Karabasken's 1st Pillared Hall after the removal of four feet of flood debris which revealed a hidden room with a shaft and two burial chambers. Karabasken's sarcophagus is in the rear of the tomb – 2016

The South Tombs of Asasif

This aerial photograph was taken from a hot air balloon in 2013. It shows the staircase and open court of Karabasken's tomb, the staircase, open court, 1st and 2nd Pillared Halls of Karakhamun's tomb, and the open court of Nesbanebdjed's tomb which was usurped by Itieru in the 26th Dynasty. Nesbanebdjed's name was discovered in 2020. The unfinished tomb of an unknown person was discovered in 2021.

The Tomb Of Karakhamun

When Dr. Pischikova found the original location of Karakhamun's burial site in 2001, the tomb barely existed. The only sign of it was a large crack in the bedrock, partially hidden under sand and garbage. The local residents stated that a family once lived in the gradually collapsing tomb and that the only inhabitable area was used as a stable until its total disintegration. The final collapse of the ceiling occurred in the 1990s due to flash floods in the area. Ultimately the staircase leading into the vestibule, the sun court and tomb itself, were buried under tons of debris whenever water flooded the land at the foot of the mountain.

These flash floods occurred dozens of times over millennia until every tomb in the Kushite necropolis was buried under flood debris more than 20 feet deep. The accumulation of wet sand caused irreparable damage to the fragile limestone structures, and the artwork carved on the ceiling, walls and pillars. Karakhamun's tomb was a victim of these frequent natural disasters until all that remained was a gaping hole where an underground temple was once constructed. To make matters worse, the residents used this site as a garbage dump.

Elena started fieldwork in the tomb of Karakhamun in the summer of 2006 without much hope of ever reconstructing it or expecting to find any surviving art. Her preliminary observations showed that the crack in the bedrock was located above the remains of the First Pillared Hall.

The tomb was built 20 feet below ground level and the entrance structures and open court had long disappeared under the houses of the village. The primary goal of the first season in 2006 was to determine if any traces of the tomb's architecture or its decorative features had survived. The onset of the excavation met with numerous difficulties, including the removal of the odiferous garbage dump, and many disappointments. After reaching the original ceiling level, about 10 feet below ground level, they realized that the ceiling collapse had brought down the tops of the pillars and walls. They dug a trench along the eastern section of the First Pillared Hall to explore the condition of the walls and pillars, but it yielded only negative information. Neither relief decoration on the walls, nor vestiges of standing pillars were visible.

Excavating the garbage pit above Karakhamun's Tomb

Early excavation of Karakhamun's Tomb

The first small fragments of relief decoration were found on the north wall almost 6.5 feet below ceiling level, but the real discovery occurred on the east wall. Divided by a door-frame, we discovered the remains of two mirror-image offering scenes of Karakhamun seated before an offering table with a procession of offering bearers performing offering rituals in front of him. Although this scene was destroyed on the south side of the wall, it was unexpectedly well preserved on the north side. Additionally, one of the most elegantly carved images on the east wall was that of a dog lying under the chair of Karakhamun.

The greatest joy of the excavation team occurred when they finally found the first image of Karakhamun. He is depicted with a broad-shouldered torso, narrow waist, heavily muscled legs, closely cropped hair, and bare feet in the fashion of the Old Kingdom. He sits on a bovine-legged chair resting on a double pedestal, with a short back and a papyrus umbel behind it, wearing a pleated kilt and broad collar. His rounded head has full cheeks, a broad nose, and a short chin—features shared by many Kushite images.

Karakhamun's facial features allow for more precise dating when they are compared to royal relief images. His slightly slanted eyes, with an elegantly carved, thin upper rim extend to a short tapered cosmetic line. The shape of Karakhamun's eyes and elongation of the neck endow his face with an elegance and sophistication that brings it closer to images of pharaoh Shebitku. The latter's well-preserved image in the chapel of Osiris-Hekadjet in Karnak displays features that may have inspired Karakhamun to emulate them.

The importance of this find was not only in its confirmation that some of the decorative art had survived, but also in the exquisite quality of the carving, demonstrating that it was one of the most beautiful Kushite tombs in the Theban necropolis.

Art elements from Karakhamun's tomb

Seated image of Karakhamun

*Partially excavated 1st Pillared Hall looking west toward the unexcavated
2nd Pillared Hall, and the Asasif Mountains in the distance*

Reconstruction Of A Pillar In The Tomb Of Karakhamun

Much of the damage done to the tomb of Karakhamun occurred in the late 20th century when the ceiling collapsed and tons of falling debris shattered the pillars and walls that once supported the ceiling. More than 34,000 fragments from the ceiling, pillars and walls were found during excavation, and our team registered, photographed and stored them in the tomb of Karabasken. During the 2010 season we reconstructed a pillar on the north side of the First Pillared Hall. The conservators joined 297 fragments of relief decoration and reinstalled 90 fragments in their original locations.

The height of the pillar as found in 2008 was below 3 feet *in situ,* with the height of the ceiling in the north-west corner at 10 feet 8 inches. Numerous fragments found around the pillar allowed us to immediately start the reconstruction of the text and the image of Karakhamun kneeling in front of Ra-Harakhty and the deities of the Hours on the ground. The reconstruction was considerably altered in 2009, as almost 80% of the text and imagery was preserved. This permitted a reconstruction *in situ.*

The first step was the consolidation of the remaining part of the pillar with steel rods, lime plaster and other conservation materials. The second step was to build a metal structure that could support the weight of the reconstructed sections of the ancient pillar. Five holes (3/4 inch in diameter and 3 feet deep) were drilled into the pillar, penetrating through it into the bedrock floor. Steel rods were inserted into the holes forming supports for a metal frame made of steel bars. The reconstructed section of the pillar, composed of ancient fragments and new limestone, would rest on the metal frame that was now firmly secured into the floor of the tomb.

We purchased large blocks of limestone and hired a stonecutter to cut and dress the stone to the dimensions given him by the conservators. We secured 20-foot-long railroad ties to build a new ramp to support the weight of the 3-ton stone blocks that were transported into the tomb by the workmen, and we rented equipment to hoist the limestone blocks into place. All of this was done under the watchful eye of the "Reise" who supervised the operations and ensured that no building materials were damaged, or workmen injured.

Four courses of limestone were built to support the fragments of the decoration and ancient fragments were attached to reveal large sections of text. Deep sockets were carved in the new limestone to receive the ancient fragments and ensure their stability and protection. The gaps were filled with lime plaster. Ultimately, the pillar was rebuilt to its original height of 10 feet and crowned with an 8-inch section of an architrave to reach the ceiling height of 10 feet 8 inches.

We reconstructed the remaining pillars, pilasters, and the walls of the tomb in 2017 and installed a temporary roof over the entire structure in 2019. The textual program of the tomb of Karakhamun consists of a very elaborate schema. Although most of the inscriptions were found in fragments in the debris, the amount of recovered information is sufficient to identify 33 chapters of the *Book of the Dead* that were placed on the walls and pillars of the tomb.

So far, the textual program of the tomb of Karakhamun may be seen as the *Book of the Hours of the Day,* starting on the northeast pillar with the First Hour of the Day, and developing east-west with three hours on each pillar. The text continues on the south pillars with the Hours of the Night starting on the southwest pillar and developing west-

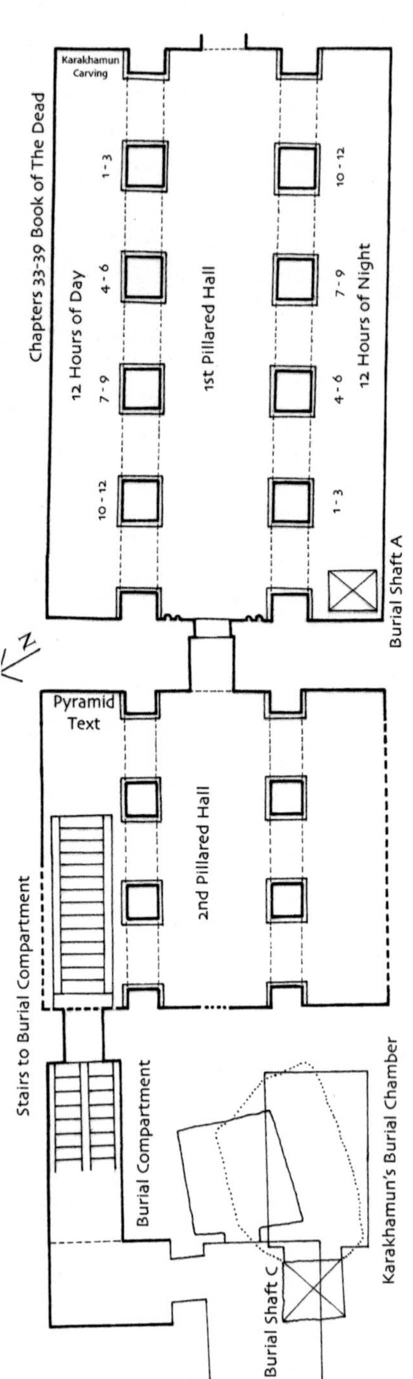

east. Therefore, in the First Pillared Hall we have a cosmic picture of the sun traveling through the day and night sky. As far as we now know, every Hour text is topped with a figure of Ra-Horakhty being adored by Karakhamun. The sides of the pillars facing the walls contain chapters from the *Book of the Dead,* and all the walls are inscribed with texts from the *Book of the Dead.*

The Second Pillared Hall is smaller than the first and is comprised of four pillars which were also inscribed with text from the *Book of the Dead.* A pair of Spanish Egyptologists working with our team made another interesting discovery as they examined the hieroglyphic inscriptions carved on the wall in front of the steps leading down to the burial compartment. After careful analysis, they concluded that the writings on the wall were copies of passages from the *Pyramid Texts* that were discovered inside of a burial chamber beneath the pyramid of Unas, the 5th dynasty king who was buried at Saqqara near the Step Pyramid of Zoser.

The *Pyramid Texts* were first recorded around 2370 BCE. and are "the oldest religious writings yet discovered in the world." Carved on the walls of the burial chamber of Unas are 236 utterances of the *Resurrection Ritual* designed to arouse the spirit of the deceased king from his grave and send it into the heavens, to the stars in the constellation of Sahu (Orion) where it would be reborn. Among the astronomical traditions of ancient Kemet, Sahu was associated with Ausar (Osiris), the *Lord of Judgment* and *Resurrection.* According to Robert Bauval and Adrian Gilbert in their groundbreaking publication, *The Orion Mystery,* "...the word for making a mummy in Ancient Egyptian was, not surprisingly, Sahu."

We found written among the Pyramid Texts in the tomb of Karakhamun, his name—followed by the phrase, *maa-kheru,* which means "true of voice." This expression dates from the Old Kingdom and is the voice of Ausar who informs the soul of the deceased at the last judgment that their statement that they have not sinned is acknowledged as true and they may be "admitted to the safety of the hereafter." These ancient writings constitute the oldest recorded references to the judgment of the soul and resurrection. Their presence inside of the tomb of Karakhamun is an indication that the people of Kush preserved and resurrected the memories of their ancient ancestors.

Karakhamun's tomb is an exquisite example of early Kushite art. With so few preserved monuments from the time of Shabaka–Shebitku, the tomb's decoration notably adds to the picture of "archaizing" stylistic trends in early Kushite tomb art based on Old Kingdom traditions and now known as the "Kushite Renaissance." The tomb demonstrates the highest quality of relief carving, defining the Kushite period as one of the most significant and glamorous periods of Kemetic culture.

Karakhamun's tomb contains more priceless works of art and sacred texts than most tombs in the area. We know this because we have, slowly but surely, brick by brick, season after season, rebuilt Karakhamun's tomb and brought it back to life.

Reconstructed pillar in Karakhamun's 1st Pillared Hall

*Workmen restoring a pillar in the 1st Pillared Hall while others
excavate and remove debris in the 2nd Pillared Hall*

Finding The Burial Chamber Of Karakhamun

During a typical excavation season, we worked at the site seven hours a day, six days a week, from 6:00 AM until 1:00 PM. We began each day at sunrise to escape the scorching desert heat of the afternoon sun. At 6:00 AM, the tomb was in the shadows and was pleasantly cool. By 8:00 AM sunlight began to illuminate the upper rim of the tomb and by 10:00 AM the sun was high enough in the sky to turn the worksite into an open-air oven. Over the course of several days, the workmen cleared debris from the Second Pillared Hall, uncovered large pieces of the collapsed tomb ceiling, the truncated remains of two pillars and dozens of fragments. By 10:30 AM the work pace slowed as the temperature inched closer to 118° Fahrenheit. I found numerous ways to keep the workmen motivated and to take our minds off the intense heat. I played practical jokes on some of the conservators and engaged in a mock shouting match with some of the older workers.

These distractions helped develop a bond of camaraderie between the work crew and me. Since I was the only person at the work site with a bald head, some of the fellows began calling me Karakhamun because of the similarities of our shaved heads. I was pleased with the comparison and as I struggled to meet ever-rising expenses and continually dwindling funds, I found myself calling on Karakhamun for assistance on more than one occasion.

One particularly hot afternoon in 2010, while I was contemplating how we could use our workforce more efficiently, I called on Karakhamun for guidance. I informed him that we were here as tomb restorers, not tomb robbers, and that the work we were doing would bring honor to his name. I petitioned Karakhamun to tell me where we could find the stairs that would lead to his burial chamber. A voice that I know was more inspiration than imagination said, *"Have the men dig there!"*, in an area near the base of a pillar the workers had recently uncovered. I asked Elena to lend me a couple of men to work in that area. She questioned my request and I said, "Elena, trust me, I've got a good feeling we will find something."

Fortunately, Elena had learned to trust my instincts and she gave me a few of her best diggers. Two days later, while working in another part of the tomb, I heard Elena shout out, "Tony, Tony, we found it. We found steps." I rushed to the site where Karakhamun had instructed

Tony at first step

me to dig and saw a pair of partially exposed steps peering up out of the earth. Everyone was filled with anticipation as we carefully began excavating the stairs wondering what we would or would not find.

I left Egypt in mid-July, shortly after the discovery of the steps, and returned to the U.S. for two weeks to secure additional funds, escort my next study tour to Egypt, and bring the next group of volunteers to work on the mission. During the interim, I received regular updates about the progress at the site. Shortly after my birthday (July 26) I received a call from Elena telling me that they found Karakhamun's burial chamber and that they would seal it off until my return so I would be the first to begin excavations inside. That was to be my birthday present.

August 13, I returned to the excavation site with my daughter Atlantis to join the new mission members. This was her fourth trip to Egypt and her first time participating in an archeological dig. During my absence the crew had cleared 14 steps that led to the burial compartment and later covered them up so they wouldn't be damaged as workers continued excavating in the Second Pillared Hall. They left a small opening through which we could access the burial compartment.

Atlantis and I arrived at the site eager to see what we would find. We crawled through the opened entrance above the covered staircase and entered a spacious burial chamber where we saw two smaller side rooms filled with debris and a 26-foot-deep shaft in the far corner. Since we didn't have a ladder long enough to enter the shaft, the workmen tied two 15-foot ladders together so we could access the main burial chamber, which was about 56 feet below ground level.

As we climbed down the ladder, we saw two burial chambers, the main one at the bottom of the shaft and the secondary one directly above it. As my daughter and I stood before the entrance of the main burial chamber, I asked her to enter first so that she would be the first African American to enter Karakhamun's burial chamber. I quickly followed behind her and what we found inside amazed us.

The main burial chamber was almost completely filled with debris with only the tops of the walls and the ceiling visible. Unfortunately, modern grave robbers had already desecrated the tomb, stripping it of its contents and filling it with debris to cover their tracks. The approximate size of the room is 16.4 feet wide x 10.8 feet long x 7.5 feet high.

The burial chamber was plastered and brightly painted with astronomical scenes. The ceiling was painted blue with yellow and red stars. The middle of the ceiling was occupied by a large figure of the

Tony and Atlantis inside Karakhamun's burial chamber

goddess Nut painted yellow with long black hair. She was surrounded by astronomical figures and deities of the southern and northern constellations. The best-preserved images of these heavenly deities were Isis-Sothis, the goddess of the star Sirius in a bark; the Big Dipper constellation depicted as a bull with a falcon-headed god Ani on the right and goddess Serket on the left; Osiris in a bark representing Orion (Sahu); and a procession of deities identified with various other planets and stars.

A group of Supreme Council of Antiquities conservators working under the supervision of the Conservation Director of Luxor examined the condition of the burial chamber decoration and found it generally stable. The weak areas that required emergency consolidation were quickly repaired. Further excavation, conservation and reconstruction of the burial chamber was undertaken in the 2011 season.

Mummified child's hand

Atlantis and I spent six days in the burial chamber labeling stone fragments from the ceiling, walls and pieces of a wooden coffin that were strewn throughout the room. Sadly, we began finding skeletal remains. Some had been stripped of their linen wrappings and discarded among the rubble inside the chamber. We found two adult skulls and fragments of a jaw, spine and pelvis, but the most surprising discovery was the mummified hand of a small child.

The sudden realization that we were quite possibly in the family burial chamber of Karakhamun, his wife and child, made our time together more meaningful. Of my 45 trips to Egypt this was, by far, my most memorable. The finding of a large, decorated tomb, plus three additional tombs inside the burial compartment at the foot of the recently excavated staircase, increased the likelihood that we had uncovered a 25th dynasty family burial site. When one considers the size of Karakhamun's tomb, the high quality of the carvings and decorations, and the number of burial chambers, it is obvious that Karakhamun was a man of considerable wealth and might possibly have been a member of the royal family.

The possibility that we had just discovered a 2700-year-old family crypt was the topic of discussion at dinner that evening. My daughter commented that our excavations in South Asasif were beginning to look like a family affair. This family tomb was re-discovered and being excavated by Dr. Pischikova and her daughter Katherine. Now it was being excavated by our family also—and an extended family of volunteers and supporters.

Atlantis inside vestibule

Tony, Katherine, Elena, and Atlantis

The excavated staircase leading to Karakhamun's vestibule

2010 Excavations in 2nd Pillared Hall (left) and 1st Pillared Hall (right)

1st Pillared Hall

2nd Pillared Hall

Part Two
The ASA Restoration Project

A Chance Encounter at South Asasif

The ASA Restoration Project evolved out of a chance meeting between Dr. Elena Pischikova and me in July 2008. I had recently arrived in Luxor, having just completed a tour of the western desert, and was awaiting the arrival of a group from the U.S. which I was to lead on a 15-day study tour of Egypt. I had several free days before my group arrived and my friend and tour guide, Abu El Naga Gabriel, introduced me to his cousin who was working with an Egyptologist who had recently made discoveries that he thought would be of interest to me.

Arrangements were made for me to meet this Egyptologist, Dr. Elena Pischikova, the following day. Abu Naga's nephew Hassan drove me to South Asasif where I met Elena who gave me a personal tour of the three tombs she had recently "rediscovered." After we were formally introduced, Elena told me of her childhood in Russia and her lifelong interest in Egypt. She told me of her joy when she received a scholarship to travel from Moscow to New York City to study Egyptian history under the tutelage of Dr. Bernard Bothmer, one of the foremost experts on Egyptian and Kushite Art of the Late Period.

Elena described her love of 25th dynasty history and art, and how her work with various museums in New York led to her heading the restoration and conservation of a 26th dynasty tomb in North Asasif. When she was not preoccupied with her primary duties, Elena spent her free time searching for the lost Kushite tombs of South Asasif, about two miles to the south. She ultimately concentrated her search on a local village where the residents had been rumored to have built their homes over undiscovered tombs and were selling newly found artifacts to tourists.

After a series of meetings with village elders, Elena was finally shown the location of the tombs of Itieru and Karabasken, which had already been pillaged by residents of the village. Based on her research of Karabasken's tomb Elena knew that the tomb of Karakhamun, which was last seen in the 1970s, was somewhere nearby, and she began excavating in an area that had recently been used as a garbage dump. After several weeks of removing tons of garbage, sand, and debris, the workers began finding evidence of a tomb.

Through their tireless efforts, Elena and her team unearthed fragments indicating that they had rediscovered the tomb of

Karakhamun. However, Elena's story took a sad turn when she told me of her inability to secure funding to continue her work and was actually discouraged from continuing her excavation. She told me that her employer and colleagues urged her to "leave it alone" and not pursue the matter because "they (Nubians) are not your people."

Because of her specialized interest in the 25th dynasty, Elena had a greater appreciation for Kushite culture than traditional Egyptologists. "The Kushites and the ancient Egyptians share a long history," Elena told me, "and black Americans have a right to know this history."

Elena was so convinced of the importance of her find that she financed the excavation herself. She withdrew funds from her 401K, and when those funds were exhausted, she used her credit cards to pay the workers' salaries and purchase materials. When her credit cards were maxed out Elena began tapping into her daughter's college fund, and after two and a half years of excavating, Elena ran out of money just as important discoveries were being made.

Elena's story was compelling, and I was impressed by her candor and determination to press on with the excavation despite mounting difficulties. She told me that many Egyptologists were reluctant to acknowledge a favorable relationship between Kush and Egypt because they have been traditionally viewed as two racially distinct groups. But she knew otherwise and felt that the tombs of Karabasken and Karakhamun could document important historical, cultural and racial relationships between the Kushites and the ancient Egyptians and could have the impact of righting a grave historical injustice. Elena said that this discovery would be as important to the African American community as it was to the Egyptological community, but she knew of no African Americans that she could appeal to for assistance.

After this brief introduction, Elena took me on a personal tour of the three tombs. I was dismayed when I saw the damage and condition of the tombs of Itieru and Karabasken.

But when I walked down into the tomb of Karakhamun I was infused with a sense of life and hope. I saw dozens of workers removing debris, teams of college students registering newly found fragments, and several conservators restoring and consolidating walls and pillars. This house of death was being revived right before my eyes.

When I was shown the recently discovered wall carving of Karakhamun his spirit moved me—I immediately understood the importance of this project, and knew that I must be involved. I made a commitment to Elena to spread the word of her discovery throughout my community and help raise funds so that this important work could continue. Ten days later I brought my study group to the site for a personal tour. Upon seeing the wonderful work taking place in the tomb, the group immediately took up a collection to help Elena meet her payroll for the week. Throughout the rest of our trip, we talked about what we could do to support the South Asasif Conservation Project. Upon our return to the U.S., we implemented a plan of action.

The 2008 study group visiting the tomb of Karakhamun

The Reise supervises the workers at Karakhamun's tomb

Asa G. Hilliard, III

The Birth of the ASA Restoration Project

My love affair with ancient Egypt began in 1977 when I saw the King Tut exhibit in Washington, D.C. At the time, I was more interested in Egyptian art than history. My interests profoundly changed when I met Ivan Van Sertima at a Black History Month presentation at Georgetown Law School in Washington, D.C. Van Sertima was discussing his book, *They Came Before Columbus: The African Presence in America.* It was during Van Sertima's talk that I learned the ancient Egyptians were Black Africans. This simple fact was as mind blowing as it was freeing.

I revisited the King Tut exhibit armed with this new historical perspective and this time I saw an entirely different exhibit. I also gained a better understanding of the role artists played in documenting and preserving history. Artisans are responsible for creating sacred and secular objects and places that preserve and restore our memories of the past.

Paintings, sculpture and jewelry help us understand how people looked and dressed. Words and images written on papyrus and carved on walls help us understand their thoughts. The excavation of monuments, temples and tombs allows us to reconstruct ancient lives and understand how people lived, died and prepared for the afterlife.

As my interest in ancient Egyptian history broadened, I met scholars and historians who taught me to appreciate the simple truth that the past is prologue and that "all history is a current event." One individual instrumental in shaping my understanding of ancient Egypt was Dr. Asa G. Hilliard, III. I met Dr. Hilliard in 1982 and our teacher/student relationship evolved into a friendship that lasted for twenty-five years.

Dr. Hilliard was an educator, psychologist and historian whose professional career spanned the globe. He received a B.A. in Psychology and an Ed. D. in Educational Psychology from the University of Denver. He taught for several years at San Francisco State University before accepting a position as superintendent of schools in Monrovia, Liberia. After several years in Liberia, Dr. Hilliard returned to San Francisco State University where his tenure as department chair, and later, Dean of Education is legendary.

As an educational consultant Dr. Hilliard worked with school districts, universities, government agencies and public advocacy organizations throughout the nation helping infuse African content into curriculums. He was also a Board-Certified Forensic Examiner and Diplomate of both the American Board of Forensic Examiners and the American Board of Forensic Medicine.

Dr. Hilliard's career as a historian and researcher is equally impressive and he viewed his role of correcting the distorted image of Africans in history as his sacred mission. He was one of the principal organizers and presenters at the 1984 Nile Valley Conference that was held at Morehouse College in Atlanta, Georgia. This historic gathering of Egyptologists and scholars from across the globe presented new findings on ancient Egypt. Dr. Hilliard also spent over thirty years leading study tours to Egypt and Ghana and was a founding member of the Association for the Study of Classical African Civilizations, an organization dedicated to researching Nile Valley history.

Dr. Hilliard was the opening keynote speaker at the 24th annual ASCAC conference that was held in Aswan, Egypt August 7-10, 2007. His informative lecture on the peopling of ancient Egypt, its science and development prompted General Samir Yussef, the Governor of Aswan, to acknowledge that he learned more about the history of Egypt listening to Dr. Hilliard, than he had learned in his entire life. Dr. Hilliard had a similar impact on anyone who heard him speak. Unfortunately, this was the last public address Dr. Hilliard ever made. He fell ill the next day and transitioned in Anwar Sadat Hospital in Cairo on August 13, 2007. News of Dr. Hilliard's passing sent shockwaves of sadness around the world as thousands learned of his sudden loss.

It was only fitting that an effort to raise funds to support the excavation of the tomb of Karakhamun be named in honor of a man who dedicated his life to raising awareness of the contributions of African people to world history. Upon consulting with Dr. Hilliard's wife Patsy, and their children, we were given their blessings to name our project in his honor—and the ASA Restoration Project was born on September 21, 2008.

What is the ASA Restoration Project?

ASA is an acronym for the **A**sa G. Hilliard **S**outh **A**sasif **Restoration Project.** Our efforts are dedicated to the "Restoration of the Kushite presence in Kemet and the preservation of the legacy of Dr. Asa G. Hilliard, III." Our primary goal is to support the work of Dr. Elena Pischikova and the South Asasif Conservation Project by raising funds and publicizing our important discoveries. The discovery of the tombs of Karabasken and Karakhamun have made it possible for the world to learn of the lives of the first known Kushite noblemen to be buried in Kemet. Telling their story made it possible to connect the 25th dynasty with their Kemetic ancestors who lived 2,000 years earlier. This knowledge is as important to the African American community as it is to the worldwide community and our involvement ensured that the excavation continued, and the information discovered was disseminated.

The ASA Restoration Project is a subsidiary of IKG Cultural Circles, which is affiliated with the IKG Cultural Resource Center in Washington, D.C. Our mission is to make history more accessible to the public by showing a correlation between ancient and contemporary history. Our goal is to help people, particularly students of all ages, learn to draw upon the historical lessons of the past to improve their lives.

The ASA Restoration Project was established as a 501 (c)(3) non-profit corporation to raise tax-deductible contributions and finance excavations in South Asasif. Since 2009, we have raised millions of dollars and recruited dozens to work on the excavation missions conducted between June and September. Volunteers spent a minimum of two weeks registering, photographing and cataloging the thousands of fragments that were used to reconstruct the tomb of Karakhamun.

The registration of newly found artifacts is a tedious and important part of any excavation. As fragments of ceilings, walls and pillars are found, each one must be numbered and recorded. A general description of each fragment (which includes measurements and a drawing) was recorded on a registration form before the object was photographed and put into storage until it was restored to its proper place inside the tomb.

Various ASA Restoration Project Volunteers

Volunteers, working in the registration tent on the perimeter of the tomb, register dozens of fragments each day. Another group of volunteers, working at our guesthouse, enter the data from the registration forms into a computer database. This redundancy allows us to have a paper, digital and photographic record of each fragment for safekeeping. Keeping the data in multiple formats also makes it easier for us to match fragments, decipher text and index data for future publications.

The funds raised by the ASA Restoration Project allowed us to pay the salaries of the workmen at the site. We employed over one hundred workers, many of whom dug through sand and debris uncovering fragments to be registered. Dozens of other workmen removed tons rubble from the worksite in large baskets. We employed a team of highly skilled conservators who consolidated the walls and pillars, in-situ, to prevent them from collapsing as they were being excavated. Other conservators rebuilt the excavated areas of the tomb with fragments from storage. We employed a foreman who supervised the work crew, and two others who supervised the conservators. Added to this mix were inspectors from the SCA who oversaw all the activity at the site. And, when the site was closed during the evening and off-season (September through April), we also paid the salaries of the men who guard the site 24/7.

Thus far, the ASA Restoration Project has raised over $2.5M which was used to pay salaries, purchase supplies, tools, surveying equipment and laptops for the South Asasif Conservation Project.

We have had a physical presence at the excavation site since 2009, and during that time we developed bonds of friendship with many of the Egyptian workmen. Volunteers of the ASA Restoration Project made personal contributions of money, T-shirts, shoes and work gloves. We've shared tea with some workers and meals with the families of others.

*Ali and Helen Salahuddin
with Elena Pischikova*

One of our volunteers, Dr. Tenesha Bazemore (a Doctor of Optometry) was able to provide medical assistance for an elderly worker recovering from cataracts and provide free medical treatment in the U.S. for the teenage son of an SCA supervisor who lost sight in one eye as the result of an automobile accident in Luxor.

We were also able to open the site to study tours visiting Egypt during the summer. The largest group to visit the site was a group of 260 youth and adults who toured Egypt under the auspices of a Philadelphia based association called the African Genesis Institute. Ali and Helen Salahuddin, the founders of the African Genesis Institute, have taken more than 3,000 youth and adults to Egypt since 1997, and they presented Dr. Pischikova with a check for $2300 in support of the excavation efforts at South Asasif. Debra Watkins, the founder of ABEN (A Black Education Network), was another generous doner who contributed over $200K to our efforts.

Through our ongoing efforts we built bridges from the past into the future by spreading good will from the U.S. to the Nile Valley. The people of Egypt demonstrated a greater affinity for African Americans after President Obama delivered a direct appeal to the Islamic world for a "new beginning" at a speech at Cairo University in June 2009. The collaborative efforts of the South Asasif Conservation Project and the ASA Restoration Project could not have come at a better time. We were given a unique opportunity to do what no other black Africans or African Americans have done in history—be directly involved in funding and participating in an excavation in Egypt. I am certain that Cheikh Anta Diop, John Henrik Clarke and Asa Hilliard were pleased and blessed our efforts.

Diop

Clarke

Kemet's Four Golden Ages

Of my 68 trips to Egypt, two have been under the leadership of Dr. Asa Hilliard. Throughout his study tours, especially during his informative evening lectures, Asa taught us that *Kemet* is the oldest name for Egypt and he often spoke of the importance of seeing indigenous people through their own cultural lens. He stressed the need to make a chronological distinction between Kemet and Egypt. *Egypt* is a Greek word that was derived from the Greek's mispronunciation of *He-ka-Ptah*—the ancient temple of Ptah that was built two thousand years before the founding of Greece. The Greeks called "He-ka-Ptah" *Aegyptos,* and this word was later used as a generic name for the entire nation after the Greek conquest of Kemet in 332 BCE.

To make this distinction more memorable, Dr. Hilliard divided the history of Kemet into Four Golden Ages. He stressed that indigenous leaders from the south founded Kemet and that each Golden Age was separated by a period of political instability and social upheaval that is referred to as an Intermediate Period. During those dark ages Kemet was often a fractured nation and ruled by regional warlords. By contrast, each Golden Age was initiated by a king from the south, who reunified the two lands of Upper and Lower Kemet, implemented massive civil works projects and presided over periods of growth and prosperity for which Kemet (now Egypt) is known.

The Four Golden Ages, as defined by Dr. Hilliard are:

1st **Dynasties 3-6**	2665 - 2160 BCE	**Old Kingdom**
2nd **Dynasties 11-1**	2040 - 1784 BCE	**Middle Kingdom**
3rd **Dynasties 18-19**	1554 - 1190 BCE	**New Kingdom**
4th **dynasty 25**	747 - 657 BCE	**Late Kingdom**

The **1st Golden Age** (the Old Kingdom) was when all pyramids were constructed and is commonly called the *Pyramid Age.* The **2nd Golden Age** (the Middle Kingdom) represents an era when many of the great wisdom texts were written and is referred to as the *Literary Age.* Following this era, Kemet suffered its first major invasion by a foreign army (the Hyksos) who gained control of the delta in the extreme north. The defeated king of Kemet retreated south and established a new capital in Waset. The **3rd Golden Age** (the New

Kingdom) was established by kings of the 18th dynasty who mounted a war of liberation and drove out the foreign invaders in the north and proceeded to establish fortifications outside of Kemet, in a region of the world now known as Palestine and Israel, in order to prevent invading hordes from coming back into their land. It was during this New Kingdom that Kemetic rulers engaged in rebuilding numerous temples throughout the country and they also began burying their rulers on the west bank of Waset in an area now known as the *Valley of the Kings, Queens and Nobles.*

After the 19th dynasty Kemet experienced a protracted period of political instability that made it susceptible to invasions by Libyans who ruled areas of the country during the Third Intermediate Period. This era of unrest ended when southern kings from Kush drove out the invading hordes and established the 25th dynasty of the Late Kingdom. This epoch represented Kemet's **4th** and final **Golden Age.** According to ancient accounts these Kushite kings saw themselves, not as invaders, but as custodians of older Kemetic traditions who were on a sacred mission to restore the land of their ancestors. They accomplished this objective by reaching two thousand years into Kemet's glorious past and bringing into the present the best that the three prior Golden Ages had to offer.

Through the process of retroactive remembrances, the 25th dynasty kings rebuilt temples and monuments throughout the country and recovered and updated many sacred texts of the Old and New Kingdoms. These Kushite kings initiated a grand renaissance and reigned over an era which historian John Henrik Clarke called Kemet's "last great walk in the sun."

One of the timeless truths of every human endeavor is that all good things must come to an end. After the fall of the 25th dynasty, Kemet was once again divided and governed by a series of weak regional rulers until the Persians gained complete control of the country in 343 BCE. Eleven years later, a Greek army, led by Alexander of Macedonia, wrested control of the nation from the Persians and ushered in an era of true "Egyptian" history. These new Greek rulers Hellenized Kemetic traditions through a dynasty of Greek kings known as the Ptolemies.

In 30 BCE., with the death of Queen Cleopatra VII, 302 years of Greek rulership came to an end when Augustus Caesar conquered Egypt and made it a province (and the breadbasket) of the Roman Empire. Under Roman, rule the history and culture of Kemet and ancient Egypt were routinely suppressed.

By royal decree of the Holy Roman Emperor Theodosius in 350 ACE the writing of hieroglyphics was banned, ancient Kemetic and Egyptian libraries were destroyed, and countless sacred texts were lost. The last recorded date of hieroglyphic inscriptions was in 394 ACE. The last Egyptian temple (on the island of Phile in Upper Egypt) was closed by the Christian Emperor Justinian in 550 ACE. After the closing of Phile Temple, the ability of read medu netcher (hieroglyphics) was lost for 1272 years – until the French linguist Champollion deciphered them in 1822.

Philae Temple

The Greco-Roman occupation of Egypt lasted over 975 years (from 332 BCE. to 646 ACE). During this period of foreign rule, men with an increasingly diminished understanding of the ancient civilization that preceded them continually reinterpreted the history, culture, art and religion of Kemet. All Greek pharaohs, and many of the Roman emperors, imitated the architecture, customs and religious traditions of the ancient founders of Kemet. After the fall of Rome, Egypt was ruled by numerous mercenaries and warlords until the Arab conquest in 646.

Egypt has remained under Arab control for over thirteen hundred years despite brief periods of colonial occupation by the Turks, French and British. The Arab Spring uprisings of 2011 led to the sudden departure of President Hosni Mubarak on February 20, and the election of Mohamed Morsi in 2012. Morsi's tenure as Egyptian President lasted until July 3, 2013, when he was ousted in a "soft" coup d'etat and replaced by general Abdel El-Sisi. Egypt now struggles to find its place in a rapidly democratizing world.

Egyptian Protester in Tahrir Square, February 2011

Statues of Kushite kings in Kerma Museum in Sudan

The Genealogy of the 25th dynasty

The excavation of Karakhamun's tomb provides us with an unprecedented opportunity to explore the genealogy of a 25th dynasty royal family and their quest to restore the land of their Kemetic Ancestors. By connecting Kemet to Kush, we are also re-connecting Kemet (Egypt) to Africa and restoring historical and cultural links that have been marginalized or ignored by numerous historians. Dr. Diop emphasized the importance of such actions when he stated:

For us to return to Egypt in every domain is the necessary condition to reconcile African civilization with history…Egypt will play the same role in the thinking and renewing of African culture that ancient Greece and Rome plays in the culture of the west.

The first Kushite ruler to fully embrace the traditions of Kemet was a king named **Alara,** who ruled around 790 BCE. Alara's successor and brother **Kashta** (whose name meant the "Kushite") led the first Kushite troops into Kemet to drive out invaders from Libya. Kashta is believed to have liberated Waset (the southern capital of Kemet), which was later called Thebes by the Greeks and is now known as Luxor. Since ancient times, Waset was called "the most select of places," and was home to Karnak Temple—the largest temple complex ever built. Karnak also houses the Temple of Amun—one of the most important deities of Kemet and Kush.

After Kashta's death, his son **Piankhy** became king of Kush and led his troops into Kemet to complete his father's mission. Piankhy

Karnak Temple on the East Bank of Luxor

journeyed to the Temple of Amun at Karnak, prayed to Amun and instructed his soldiers to purify themselves in the sacred lake of the temple before engaging the enemies of their Ancestors. Piankhy's army vanquished all their foes as they marched to the delta of Lower Kemet. After having successfully united the two lands of Upper and Lower Kemet, Piankhy returned to Kush and recorded his accomplishments on a "Victory Stela" at the Temple of Amun in Gebel Barkal—which was said to be the ancestral home of the ancient deity Amun.

Egyptologists recognize Piankhy as the founder of Kemet's 25th dynasty. Upon his death Piankhy was succeeded by his brother **Shabaka** who marched into Kemet to drive out the Libyans who had regained control of Lower Kemet. To prevent further incursions, Shabaka ruled Kemet from its former northern capital of *Menefer* (Memphis) and demonstrated his desire to restore the traditions of his Ancestors by assuming the Old Kingdom throne name of *Neferkare*. Shabaka followed the tradition of restoring the past as his brother and father had done before him. Their collective actions set in motion an act of "retroactive remembrances" which Egyptologist Jan Assmann referred to as Egypt's (and the world's) first renaissance.

Shabaka continued the tradition of reaching into Kemet's golden past by having his scribes rewrite an ancient document called the "Memphite Theology" that was said to be "worm eaten" when it was found in the library of the Temple of Ptah. That document survives today on a large slab of basalt that is displayed in the British Museum labeled "the Shabaka Stone," and is a record of one of the oldest creation stories ever written.

The Shabaka Stone

When he died, Shabaka was succeeded by his nephew **Shebitku** (a son of Piankhy) who also took a throne name from the Old Kingdom, *Djedkare*, and a name from the New Kingdom, *Khaemwaset*—which means, "Crowned in Waset."

Upon his death, Shebitku was succeeded by his brother **Taharqa** who built numerous temples in Kush and restored others in Kemet. One of his greatest restoration projects was the expansion of the sacred lake in Karnak and the erection of ten columns at the entrance to Karnak Temple. The columns were built to a height of almost 21 m (70') and were the tallest ever constructed in Kemet. Unfortunately, only one column has survived the ravages of time and man.

The sacred lake at Karnak Temple

Taharqa also holds the distinction of being the only Egyptian pharaoh who is mentioned by name in the Bible. Two references to Taharqa can be found in the Old Testament text of Isaiah 37: 8-9, and 2nd Kings 19: 8-9.

When Taharqa died in 664 BCE., his nephew **Tanutamun** inherited a severely weakened nation that was under constant assault from a vastly superior Assyrian army. Tanutamun had a grand vision of reconquering all of Kemet, which was recorded in a dream stela written in a style with literary allusions to the Old Kingdom text known as *The Teachings of Ptah-hotep*, regarded as the oldest book in the world.

Tanutamun's military campaign was reminiscent of that of his father Piankhy, and the priests in each town he conquered greeted him as a liberator. Upon defeating the Assyrian army and their Kemetic collaborators in the north, Tanutamun offered prayers of thanks to Amun for empowering him to fulfill his vision. His prayers included the following acknowledgement:

My lord is with me, this sublime god,
Amun-Re, lord of Karnak, who resides in Gebel Barkal

Unfortunately, Tanutamun's victory was short lived. The Assyrian army launched a major offensive and won a decisive battle in Lower Kemet, and every battle thereafter, on their long and bloody march south to Waset. The Assyrians were the first foreign army to successfully invade Kemet's southern capital. They destroyed the city, reduced Karnak to ruins and drove the Kushites out of Kemet.

With the fall of the 25th dynasty the Assyrian army established Pasmmeticus I as the first ruler of Kemet's 26th dynasty. It was during this Late Period of Kemetic history that we find the beginnings of a concerted effort to erase the Kushite presence in Kemet.

In total, five 25th dynasty kings, from Piankhy to Tanutamun, ruled Kemet for almost a century. They were all members of the same royal household, and more than likely, adhered to the well-established tradition of appointing family members to important leadership posts throughout the country. To the best of our knowledge, Karabasken and Karakhamun were the first Kushite nobles buried in Kemet. It is quite possible that Karabasken (the mayor of Waset) and Karakhamun (the first aq priest of Amun at the Temple of Amun in Karnak) were members of the royal family. The evidence for this may lie buried in the sands of South Asasif, waiting to be rediscovered in the not-too-distant future.

Statues of Kushite kings in Louvre Museum

Part Three
Highlights of Fourteen Years of Excavations
(2008 – 2021)

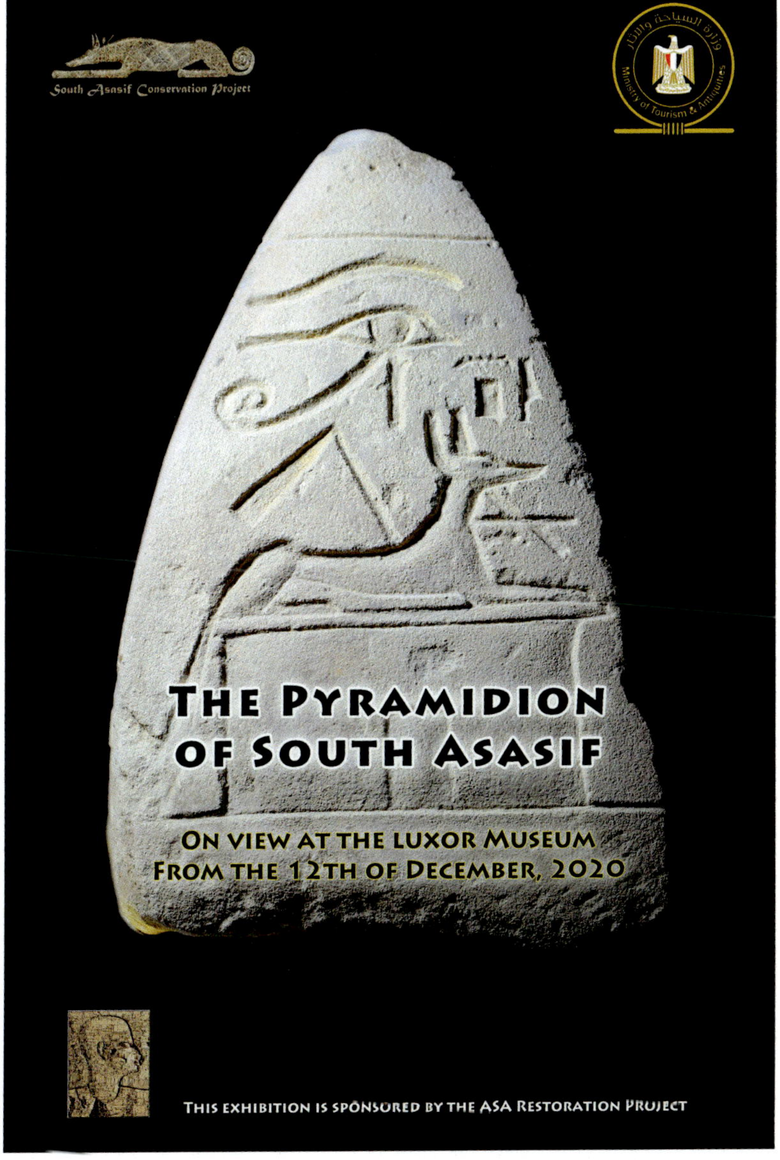

Excavation Highlights

The following discoveries underscore the significant contributions of the 25th dynasty:

- Karakhamun's tomb is the first fully decorated large Kushite tomb built in the Theban necropolis. The exquisite quality of relief carving found there demonstrates that this Kushite tomb was one of the most beautiful in the Theban necropolis, if not in all of Egypt.

- While excavating the superstructure of Karakhamun's tomb we discovered the footprint of three mudbrick pylons. The first was at the steps leading into the sun court. The second as at the entrance to the First Pillared Hall, and the third at the entrance to the Second Pillared Hall. The presence of pylons indicated that this structure was designed as a temple-tomb, a temple where priests of Amun could gather, within the tomb of their colleague Karakhamun, to honor his life and preserve the legacy of their Ancestors.

- The temple-tomb architects introduced innovative design elements in the Late Period. They enhanced the spirit door by adding a divine niche, and a surrounding corridor imitating the water-filled tomb of Ausar in Abydos.

- It is the first known tomb to reform the grid system by replacing the 18-square grid with the 21-square grid that dominated the art of the Late Period.

- It is the first known private tomb to adopt traditional subjects of royal tomb decoration such as *the Books of the Hours of Day and*

A rendering of Karabasken's Temple-Tomb with pylons and pyramid

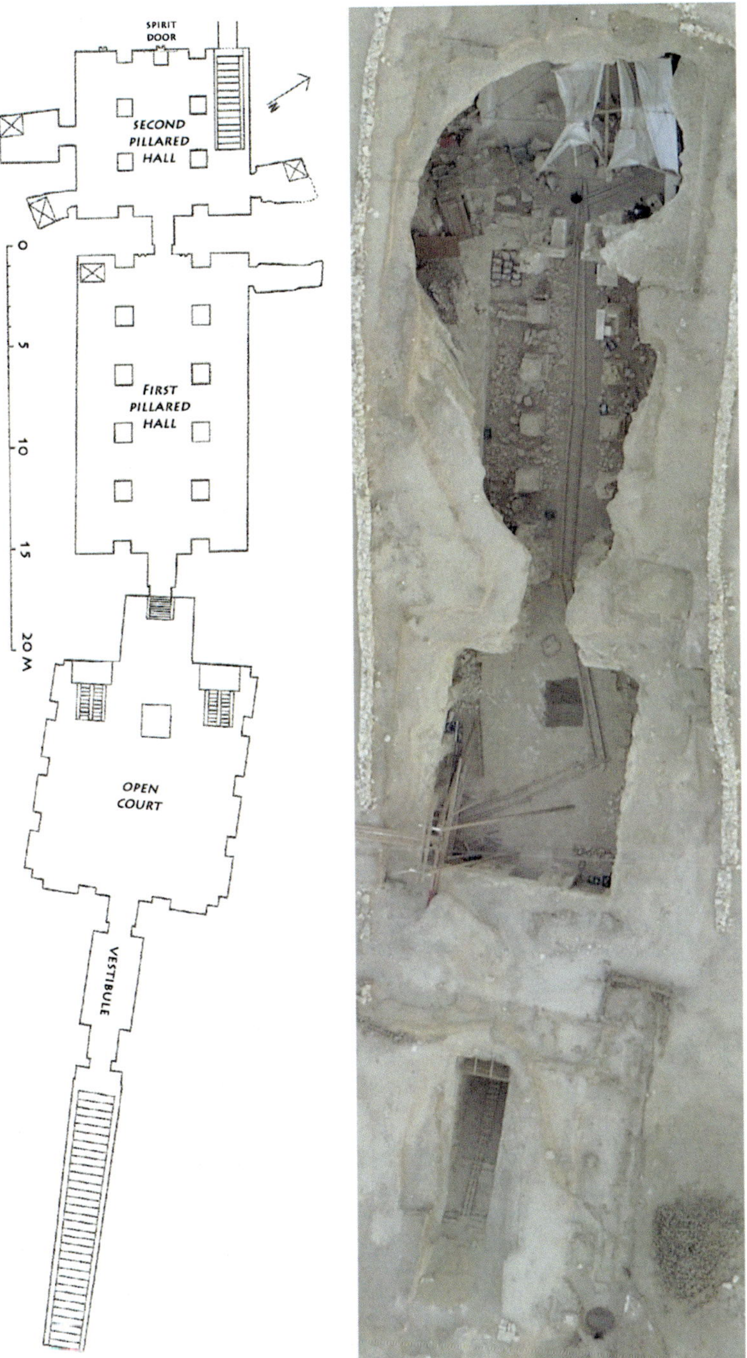

Floorplan (left) and aerial view (right) of Karakhamun's Temple-Tomb

Night and placed the text on eight pillars—three Hours on each pillar. This example was often followed in later Kushite and 26th dynasty tombs.

- The north wall in the Second Pillared Hall was inscribed with Pyramid Text Utterances 25, 73, 74 and 77, and decorated with a wide painted frieze of sacred oil jars and tools for the Opening of the Mouth ceremony.

- The discovery of Karakhamun's elaborately decorated burial chamber and three undecorated burial chambers.

- Our discoveries were showcased in three exhibitions at the Luxor Museum where we displayed an assortment of artifacts discovered in over a decade of excavations.

Pyramid Text in Second Pillared Hall

Canopic jars of Aminerdis, 2018

South Asasif Journey Through Time exhibit, 2019

Sandstone pyramidion found in open court of Nesbadnebdjed in 2020

Sankofa in the Asasif Necropolis

Art and architecture are two critical means of studying the past and gaining a meaningful understanding of the history and culture of a people. A comprehensive study of the art and architecture of ancient Egypt has yielded invaluable information about this ancient civilization, the lives of the people who settled in the Nile Valley thousands of years ago, and the traditions they passed on to posterity.

South Asasif Mountains

Our team had the opportunity to exhibit some of our discoveries in three exhibitions in the Luxor Museum. The second exhibition was titled *The South Asasif Necropolis: Journey Through Time.* It represented a significant contribution towards expanding our understanding of Egypt's 25th dynasty and the Kushite nobles who were buried in the most famous necropolis in ancient times. The exhibition opened on September 8, 2019, and consists of over one hundred meticulously curated artifacts discovered by the South Asasif Conservation Project (SACP) in our excavations of the tombs of Karabasken, Karakhamun and Nesbanebdjed.

This new installation at the Luxor Museum paid homage to the craftsmanship of the artisans who designed and constructed these 2800-year-old tombs, and the artifacts found within them. It also honored the outstanding work of the SACP team members who carefully excavated these hallowed spaces. Our team found more than 34,000 fragments during the excavation of Karakhamun's temple-tomb; some of them were included in the exhibition. Cleaning and examining each artifact yielded important details about the object and its composition; the artist and their technique; and the relationship of that artifact to the space around it.

For thousands of years the aesthetics of ancient Egyptian architecture and visual arts have fired the imagination of artisans whose works have, in turn, influenced millions of people around the world. Studying the art and architecture of the past gives us greater insight into the culture and traditions we have inherited – and those we will pass on to our descendants. It would be fair to say that "Today's architecture and today's visual arts bend towards the future carrying the influence of ancient Egypt (with) them."

In addition to curating three exhibitions at the Luxor Museum (the first being the 2018 installation of the canopic jars discovered in the temple-tomb of Karabasken, and the third in 2020 when we displayed the pyramidion discovered in the courtyard of Nesbanebdjed), the SACP also organized two conferences themed: *Thebes in the First Millennium BC,* in 2012 and 2016. These conferences attracted an international gathering of archeologists actively excavating and or restoring temples and tombs on the east and west banks of Luxor. Both conferences featured keynotes by highly respected 25th and 26th dynasty experts, and field trips to view ongoing work at Karnak Temple and several tombs in South and North Asasif.

This chapter focuses on discoveries made in 2016 during my visit to the tombs of Sheshonq and Padiamenopet located in North Asasif near Deir el-Bahari (the Temple of Hatshepsut). Of particular note was a distinctive "double heart-spiral" pattern painted on the ceiling of the vestibules of the aforementioned 25th and 26th dynasty tombs. These patterns were intriguing because both incorporated within their design an art element similar to the "Sankofa" adinkra symbol used by the Akan people of Ghana and Ivory Coast since the late nineteenth century.

According to *The Adinkra Dictionary,* by W. Bruce Willis, "Adinkra literally means, 'saying good-bye (farewell) to the dead'" and it "implies a philosophical message that one conveys when mourning during a funeral or the post-burial memorial. There are approximately seventy symbols, sometimes referred to as the core symbols, which reflect the philosophy, religious beliefs, social values, and political history of the Akan people."

Willis stated, "Adinkra symbols are used by a grieving person to convey a message to be taken into the 'afterlife' by the departing soul." There are numerous variations of the Sankofa symbol, with slightly different meanings associated with each one, but Sankofa essentially means, "to go back to the past to gain knowledge in order to build for the future."

Kemet, 7th century BCE

Ghana, 19th century

SANKƆFA
(sang-ko-fah)

literally :

GO BACK TO FETCH IT

Symbol of the wisdom of learning from the past to build for the future

Proverb: *"Se wo were fi na wo sankɔfa a yenkyi."* (It is not a taboo to return and fetch it when you forget.)
   Sankofa is a constant reminder that past experience must be a guide for the future. Learn from or build on the past.

The artistic similarity of the heart shaped Sankofa sign and the double heart-spiral symbols on the ceilings of the tombs of Sheshonq and Padiamenopet was an unexpected discovery with profound historical and cultural implications. Understanding that the Akan Sankofa symbol was a message created by the living for the deceased to carry into the afterlife and finding a similar symbol (that pre-dated it by at least 2500 years) painted on the ceiling of two Egyptian tombs, demanded further investigation.

The tombs of Sheshonq and Padiamenopet in the ancient Theban necropolis are over 2500 miles east of the Akan burial grounds of Ghana and Ivory Coast. Was there a cultural transference of artistic and burial traditions between people in East and West Africa? But before this question can be sufficiently answered one must first investigate the origin, evolution, and diffusion of the "double heart-spiral" symbol throughout the Nile Valley.

Flinders Petrie, considered by many as the father of modern Egyptian archaeology, pointed out that, "The spiral, or scroll, is one of the greatest elements of Egyptian decoration: it is only second to the lotus in importance, and shares with that the origin of a great part of the ornament of the world. The source of the spiral and its meaning are alike uncertain."

New research on the topic was presented, almost half a century later, by Helene Kantor in her 1945 Ph.D. dissertation at Chicago's Oriental Institute. Kantor stated, "...the double heart-spiral, common today on wrought-iron fences" was first encountered "in Middle Kingdom tombs at Qau, Meir and Assiut."

Maria Shaw updated Kantor's research in the 1970 article *Ceiling Patterns from the Tomb of Hepzefa*. Shaw declared, "Well-defined spiraliform patterns first appear in Egyptian art in the Middle Kingdom, mainly as scarab designs and, in a limited extent, as painted decoration on ceilings of certain XIIth dynasty rock-cut tombs belonging to important nomarchs of provinces in Middle Egypt. Since such patterns are foreign to Egyptian decorative tradition...and since on the contrary they are common in Crete, where they appear as early as the EM II period (2900 – 2300 BCE), they have attracted the attention of scholars particularly concerned with contacts in the Aegean in this early period. This research has been summarized and brought to completion in a study by Miss H. Kantor."

Drawing on Helene Kantor's research, Maria Shaw concluded that, "...the heart-shaped motif seems to have been transmitted to Egypt early in or a little prior to the MM I period (2160-1600 BCE)...

*Illustration of double heart-spiral pattern on the ceiling
of the 18th dynasty tomb of Ramose*

the specific use of the basic motif and its translation into a potentially endless surface pattern... should be attributed to the Egyptian adoption."

The issue of artists living in one culture, and throughout different times in history, "adopting" or being influenced by the work of local or foreign artist is quite common. Artists have always been influenced by their antecedents and their contemporaries, but creative artists do more than adopt the creative work of others, they innovate and transform old ideas into something unique while sometimes retaining elements of the original design. Ms. Shaw acknowledged this fact in observing that, "Hepzefa's artist certainly showed great inventiveness in rearranging and elaborating upon a simple motif to create brilliant new decorative schemes in which the constituent parts are often hardly discernible. It is also to his credit that, while variety was achieved, a certain uniformity and harmony was maintained throughout the entire ceiling decoration."

True art inspires, and while some artistic styles go out of fashion, others are lost but never forgotten. Some styles re-emerge as they are discovered by a new generation of artists who create new designs with art elements that are hundreds or thousands of years old.

Such was the case with the double heart-spiral which was first documented in Egypt in the 12th dynasty (1938 – 1756 BCE), then disappeared for about 200 years, then reappeared in the 18th dynasty (1479 – 1426 BCE) and was discovered in the tomb of Menkheperresoneb and on the ceiling of the tombs of Antef, Neferhotep and Ramose.

Bowl with running spiral decoration

18th dynasty artisans created a unique feature in their modifications of the double heart-spiral by creating "...continuous lines of spiral patterns... placed side by side, and other patterns developed in the spaces between them." New research suggests that this innovative design element may have been introduced into Egypt by artists from Kush.

The Boston Museum of Fine Arts has in its collections (but not on display) an exquisite work of art described as a "bowl with running spiral decoration" made of "low-fired Nile alluvial clay" whose provenance has been traced to the Eastern Deffufa in Kerma and was made during the "Classic Kerma" period between 1700 and 1550 BCE. This date suggests that this exemplary piece of Kerma pottery was created in Kush sometime between the 13th and 18th dynasties in Kemet.

The double heart-spiral disappeared again, for about 700 years, before reappearing in the 25th dynasty when it was found in the tombs of Sheshonq and Padiamenopet. Now that we know this pattern was used in Kush in the 17th century BCE it raises questions as to whether artists from Kush brought this design back into Kemet nearly a thousand years later?

It is our hope that these and other questions will be answered through the ongoing work of the South Asasif Conservation Project as more ancient artifacts are found and restored in the Asasif necropolis. It is through the ongoing work of the SACP that we have come into possession of new and exciting information about the Kushite presence in Kemet. The knowledge gained from our research deepens and expands our understanding of "Thebes in the First Millennium BC," as it answers many questions and poses new ones.

After more than a decade of excavations at the temple tombs of Karabasken, Karakhamun and Nesbanebdjed, we now know they were the first Kushite tombs discovered, in the first Kushite necropolis on the West Bank of Luxor, Egypt. Our work in South Asasif has uncovered artistic and architectural innovations that had previously been attributed to the 26th dynasty. Evidence of the adaptation and expansion of these artistic and architectural innovations can be found in the late 25th dynasty tombs of Montuemhat and Padiamenopet in North Asasif.

Both tombs represent some of the finest examples of archaism in Egyptian history and are some of the crowning achievements of 25th dynasty artisans.

Egyptologist Jan Assman, author of *The Mind of Egypt,* considers the 25th dynasty a "genuine renaissance" in which "a new construction of cultural time emerged" and "references to the past took place on a scale that was completely unprecedented in Egyptian history and certainly merits being called a renaissance." Assman described the 25th dynasty as a time when, "...the past is not simply present but has to be brought forth by retroactive reference," and that "no other period in Egyptian history had a past of such richness."

The works produced by 25th dynasty artists, scribes and architects engaging in "retroactive references" is the embodiment of the Akan concept of Sankofa. These artists went back two thousand years to fetch the best of the knowledge of the ancient past, they updated and refined that knowledge and used it to create a sacred landscape that would inspire generations thousands of years in the future. It is in the tomb of Padiamenopet (built in the first millennium BCE) that I observed (in the second millennium ACE) a double heart-spiral pattern similar to that produced on a bowl in Kerma (in the seventeenth millennium BCE). That is evidence of Sankofa.

The little-known tomb of Padiamenopet has been described by Egyptologist Claude Traunecker as the "largest tomb in Egypt." Its design, scope and scale are more elaborate than some of the royal tombs in the Kings Valley on the western side of the Asasif Mountains. We do not know much of Padiamenopet other than he was a Lector Priest who Traunecker theorizes was, "an intellectual and scholar" and an "advisor to the Kushite rulers Taharqo and Tantamani."

Padiamenopet's tomb is comprised of 23 rooms and some of the walls are inscribed with sacred texts dating back to the Old Kingdom – over two thousand years earlier. It has been suggested by Traunecker that this tomb "functioned as a kind of underground library, a repository of ancient funerary literature for the use of scholars and the curious."

An extensive epigraphic study of Padiamenopet's tomb was conducted

Padiamenopet, 25th dynasty Lector Priest and scholar

by Traunecker and his colleague, Isabelle Regen, who found an interesting text which welcomes scholars and visitors (ancient and modern) with these words:

O living ones,O those who are upon earth, those who were born and those who will be born...

those who walk through the necropolis in order to entertain oneself, those who seek all kind of formulas, may they enter to this tomb, in order that they may see what is in it,

Amun-Re, Lord of the Thrones of the Two Lands lives for you, (if you) adore the god, recite the offering formula in order to make this monument complete, may you make grow that which decays.

Thus, an invitation to come to Asasif to admire the work of 25th dynasty artisans, was extended to us over 2500 years ago. We came. We excavated and investigated. We shared our findings in publications, conferences, and exhibitions. We are adding our voices to the choir of Ancestral voices still echoing through time, inviting the world to come and admire the tombs of North and South Asasif so that they will *"Take pride in their past glories, and use such truths to move into the future."*

This is Sankofa in the Asasif necropolis.

Tony with conservators

Sankofa Symbols in Kush and Kemet

Kerma, Kush 1600 BCE

Waset, Kemet 700 BCE

Karanog, Kush 250 CE

A search for Sankofa symbols in Kush has revealed a "Bowl with Bird Decoration" that was found in a grave in Karanog in 1908. The object was described as "a bird looking backward" for which there were "no Meroitic parallels." It is an ancient precursor to the Sankofa Bird images currently used in Ghana as illustrated on page 75 of this publication.

Part Four

Recovering And Preserving Historical Memory

Why Kemet Matters

The French philosopher Voltaire described history as "the fable agreed upon." And if it is true that the victors in any military conflict write history, then one must take this into account when interpreting the history of Kemet. When studying Kemet (or ancient Egypt) we must ask ourselves, "through whose historical lens are we viewing this ancient land—the African, Greek, Roman, Coptic, Arab, French, British, German or American?" Each people (foreign or domestic) have interpreted 6,000 years of ancient history through their own personal and cultural lens which inhibited or enhanced what they saw and understood.

Egyptology is a field of study that is less than 250 years old. One erroneous belief that is consistently repeated is that "the 25th dynasty is the only period in Egyptian history when *Black Pharaohs* ruled Egypt." Such a statement is historically disingenuous because it implies that of Egypt's 30 dynasties, only one was ruled by Blacks. This attempt to restrict Black rulership of Kemet to the period of the Kushite kings is no different than the geographical and political efforts to remove Egypt from Africa and relocate it in the Middle East. Another often repeated false narrative is that Africans had no history prior to their enslavement by Arabs and Europeans beginning in the 7th century.

Why is it that one must prove that Egypt is in Africa and that ancient African rulers were indigenous "Black" Africans? Similar questions are not asked of Europeans or Asians even though the anthropological and genetic evidence confirms that the first humans emerged in Africa over 200,000 years ago and migrated throughout Asia, Europe and eventually populated every country on earth.

Accepted truths should stand or fall based upon valid scientific evidence and should never be decided by commission or omission. The English artist William Blake said, "When I tell any truth, it is not for the sake of convincing those who do not know it, but for the sake of defending those that do." It is in that spirit that the ASA Restoration Project seeks to preserve the legacy of Dr. Asa Hilliard by sharing historical truths that are self-evident to all who choose to view the data objectively.

The act of examining African history and culture through the lens of indigenous African people has been viewed negatively by others who have profited from creating historically inaccurate perceptions of African people and projecting these false perspectives onto their descendants. I have often said that if the book of African history were a book of a thousand pages, the story of our enslavement would begin on page 996 and would only be two pages long. I have committed my life to documenting the missing pages of African and world history.

Every people have a moral obligation to become custodians of their ancestral inheritance. W.E.B. DuBois clearly understood this when he coined the word "Afrocentric" in 1962, as did Molefi Asante when he introduced the word "Afrocentricity" in 1980. Both scholars understood the importance of becoming the agents of their cultural narrative and not depending on others to define them. This is the greatest expression of freedom and Ancestral Intelligence. It is an appropriate response to the African proverb: "Until the lion tells his story, the tale of the hunt will always favor the hunter."

Since 2022, there has been a dramatic uptick in state sponsored anti Afrocentric sentiments in Egypt. In February 2023 a Kevin Hart concert in Cairo was cancelled because of rumors that he claimed his ancestors were, "kings and queens in Egypt." Four months later a Netflix documentary on *Cleopatra*, starring a mixed-race British actress, was met with condemnation by Egyptian media and a host of Egyptian politicians and academicians.

In February 2022, certain elements within the Egyptian government, and the Ministry of Tourism and Antiquities, became suspicious of my "Afrocentric" activities and revoked my security clearance, thus preventing me from engaging in activities in South Asasif. My security clearance was restored in July 2022, but after a brief investigation it was revoked again in 2023 and 2024. Currently I am not allowed to participate in or fund activities of the South Asasif Conservation Project in Egypt.

Such restrictions were not limited to people of African descent. In 2023, the Leiden Museum in the Netherlands and the Metropolitan Museum in New York City were banned from excavations in Egypt because both museums curated exhibitions on African Americans and ancient Egypt which the Egyptian government deemed "Afrocentric."

It currently appears that any individual or institution that has the audacity to suggest that people of African ancestry had anything to do with the civilization of ancient Egypt will not be allowed to work in Egypt. Interestingly, there has been no effort to restrict "Afrocentric" groups from traveling to Egypt, but their tour leaders are restricted from discussing ancient Egyptian history with groups in temples, tombs or museums. In other words, African Americans are allowed to travel to Egypt to spend their money, but they are not allowed to discuss the history of Africans in Egypt in public spaces.

I have found it difficult to continue traveling to Egypt while such restrictions persist and have decided to suspend my study tours and the operations of the ASA Restoration Project in Luxor until a reasonable climate of acceptance returns.

What does this mean for the future of the ASA Restoration Project?

The stated objective of the ASA Restoration Project was to document the Kushite presence in Kemet and preserve the legacy of Dr. Asa G. Hilliard, III. Over the past fifteen years we have accumulated a wealth of knowledge about the 25th dynasty. Moving forward, this information will be shared in presentations, publications and documentaries to increase public knowledge of the history of Kemet, Kush, Nile Valley civilizations, and the impact of people "from the Nile to the Niger" on neighborhoods around the world. This information will be disseminated via the domestic application of the ASA Restoration Project and is a perfect way to preserve and amplify the legacy of Dr. Hilliard. This comes at a time when the teaching of African and African American history is being banned in the United States, and hard-fought civil rights are being rolled back by state legislatures and the U.S. Supreme Court. Now more than ever we must be fortified by our history.

As with the *Egypt on the Potomac Field Trip of Washington, DC,* which I created in 1986, I have documented the presence of ancient Egyptian and Nile Valley art, architecture and symbolism in Chicago, Indianapolis, New York, Cleveland, London, Paris, Rome and other cities around the world. Just as Karakhamun and his contemporaries reached into the past to define themselves and preserve their legacy for future generations, we are in a unique position to do the same.

The ASA Restoration Project will live on through new programs and activities. To paraphrase Padiamenope, the 25th dynasty priest who lived 2700 years ago:

Amun-Re lives for you,
If you remember him,
He will give life to that which once existed.

These echoes from the past are an ever-present reminder of the spirit of Sankofa. It is by continuously engaging in "retroactive references" that we become the vessels through which Ancestors, live, speak and do their best work. It is a promise Amen-Re (the living image of the Creator) made to his children many millennia ago. It is an obligation we the living are compelled to learn and pass on to our descendants. Fulfillment of these obligations is the best example of Ancestral Intelligence. The application of which helps us progress from Sankofa to Kofa by studying and analyzing the past (Sankofa) and crafting a future based upon the application of Ancestral wisdom (Kofa).

Sankofa symbol from Ivory Coast

Afterword

I have spent the past forty-seven years studying, teaching, writing and talking about ancient Egyptian history. During that time, I made sixty-eight trips to Egypt, conducted over thirty-five study tours while funding and participating in excavations for fifteen years. One question that frequently comes up during presentations and interviews is, "How did a Black kid from the West Side of Chicago wind up excavating tombs on the West Bank of Luxor?"

That's a question I have frequently asked myself as I have reflected on the last five decades of my life. Like most people, I was introduced to ancient Egypt in elementary school and my fascination grew each time I saw a documentary on Egypt or a film with an Egyptian theme. I can honestly say that my understanding of ancient Egypt deepened and was profoundly shaped by the six Ancestors to whom this book is dedicated: Ankh Mi Ra (James Laws), Asa Hilliard, Abu Naga, Ivan Van Sertima, Patricia Newton and Runoko Rashidi. Their names are listed in the order of their ascension into Ancestorhood but my interactions with them varied at different times.

I met Ivan Van Sertima on February 21, 1977. That date is etched in my mind because that's when Ivan informed me (and everyone attending his lecture in the Georgetown Law Center Auditorium) that the ancient Egyptians were Black. That statement blew my mind because, while I knew Egypt was in Africa, I had never been told, or taught, that they were (Black) African.

Van Sertima was one of the principal organizers of the Nile Valley Conference, which was held at Morehouse College, September 26-30, 1984. This four-day event featured a host of historians, psychologists, Egyptologists, theologians, mathematicians, attorneys, educators and physicians, who interpreted aspects of ancient Egyptian history from their professional perspectives. The presenters were Black and White, and each agreed that the ancient Egyptians were indigenous Africans. The keynote presenter was to have been the great Senegalese physicist, polymath and Egyptologist Cheikh Anta Diop but he was unable to attend due to mechanical problems with his aircraft.

The *Nile Valley Conference* marked a definitive turning point in my life. While sitting in the audience listening to each speaker, I knew what I wanted to do with the rest of my life. I made a commitment to learn everything I could about Kemet (the Land of the Blacks) and

Participants in the Nile Valley Conference

share that knowledge with anyone who would listen. Van Sertima, Asa Hilliard and Charles Finch were the main conference organizers and I was blessed to form meaningful relationships with them and bring them to Washington, DC for presentations and interviews. Asa took me under his wing and provided the model for my study tours to Egypt. He wrote the introduction to my first book, *From the Browder File,* as well as the introduction to *Let the Ancestors Speak* by Ankh Mi Ra.

I met Ankh Mi Ra at one of the lectures I sponsored in Washington, DC for visiting scholars. We quickly formed a friendship centered around our mutual interests in Nile Valley and West African history. Ankh had the unique honor of hosting Theophile Obenga in his home for several months. Obenga is the Congolese Egyptologist, linguist and historian who co-presented with Diop at the 1974 Cairo Symposium and proved that the ancient Egyptians were Black. Obenga and Diop wrote extensively on the vestiges of hieroglyphics that exist within contemporary West African languages. Obenga taught Ankh Hieroglyphics (Medu Netcher) while living in his home, and Ankh became my personal consultant whenever I needed text translated or an interpretation of a Kemetic word, symbol or concept. Ankh and I had many discussions about the literal and spiritual meaning of hieroglyphic texts. I learned from these conversations that a deeper understanding of hieroglyphics can only be achieved by understanding their relationship to the people of Kemet, their social norms, psychology, geography and sacred science.

Ankh Mi Ra passed 43 days before Asa Hilliard, and the loss of these two Brothers within a relatively short period of time left a gaping hole in my soul.

Patricia Newton was a brilliant psychiatrist who knew and worked with Ankh, Asa, Finch, Van Sertima, Frances Welsing, Wade Nobles, Na'im Akbar, Richard King and a host of noted and highly respected "Afrocentric" scholars. Dr. Newton informally adopted me as her little brother because we shared so many common traits – we were only children, we were Leos, we were born in the Midwest and we both settled in the Washington, DC area. She taught me about higher brain function, neuroanatomy, melanin sciences and African spirituality, and we made numerous trips to Egypt and Ghana together.

Dr. Newton was extremely adept at identifying the cultural and spiritual traditions linking East and West Africa and she had been initiated in several indigenous spiritual systems. It is quite rare to find these traits in a western trained physician. Newton was also well grounded in Eastern wholistic and philosophical traditions which gave her a unique advantage when addressing psychological and social issues unique to people of African ancestry. One of her areas of expertise was identifying the impact of enslavement on African Americans and she was the first social scientist to coin the phrase "Post Traumatic Slavery Disorder." Newton often spoke of the epigenetics of enslavement and said, "The Africans who got on the slave ships were genetically and psychologically different than the Africans who got off the slave ships."

While working at John Hopkins Hospital in Baltimore, Dr. Newton identified the region in the brain where "Ancestral memories" reside. This is the doorway to the unconscious (spiritual) mind which her colleagues, and fellow psychiatrists, Frances Welsing and Richard King often spoke and wrote about. Dr. Newton taught me how to access knowledge buried within my spirit and how to see the world through new eyes and observe things hidden in plain sight. To say that she expanded my mind is a profound understatement.

Runoko Rashidi was another kindred spirit and fellow Leo. We were both autodidacts and our interest in African history was kindled by our first encounter with Ivan Van Sertima. Runoko wrote and edited more articles in Van Sertima's prestigious publication *Journal of African Civilization* than any other contributor. Runoko was one of the presenters at the Nile Valley Conference and he was also an authority on the African presence in early Asia. Throughout his career Runoko conducted study tours to more than 130 countries and he documented the "world-wide African presence."

Sadly, Runoko Rashidi died in Egypt – fourteen years after the death of Asa Hilliard. Both men died while on study tours and their sudden passing reminded me of the inevitability of death and responsibility of the living to ensure that the memory of our Ancestors lives on after they were gone.

Ankh Mi Ra, Asa Hilliard, Ivan Van Sertima, Patricia Newton and Runoko Rashidi devoted their lives to teaching people of African descent of Ancestors who time and history had forgotten. I am proud to have known these wise souls and to have called them my friends. Their dedication to reviving, writing and teaching the missing pages of African history added immeasurable value to my life, and prepared me for my encounter in the Western Desert with my Egyptian tour guide, friend and brother Abu El Naga Gabriel.

Journey in the Western Desert

Abu Naga and I worked together for twenty-one years. He was recognized as one of the top guides in Egypt and worked with me from 1988 until 2009. I featured Abu Naga in the introduction of my book *Nile Valley Contributions to Civilization* where he discussed African American's interest in ancient Egyptian history. In many respects Naga was more than a tour guide, he was an intelligent, enterprising soul, with an effervescent personality which made him beloved by everyone he met. He literally and figuratively opened doors for me in Egypt. Naga introduced me to Egyptian archeologists in Cairo, Saqqara and Luxor and with his seemingly endless connections he was able to get me into tombs that were not open to the public.

Abu Naga invented and popularized tours to the Western Desert, a vast deserted region between Cairo and Luxor that is connected by the Bahiriya, Farafra, Dakhla and Kharga Oases. Within this desolate sea of sand were dozens of ancient Egyptian, Greek and Roman towns, temples and tombs that were built between 2200 BCE and 500 AD. This tour is not for the faint of heart. It is accessible only by 4-wheel drive vehicles, has less than stellar accommodations, and requires camping out in the desert. Naga begged me to do the tour because of sites he wanted me to see–but I resisted for several years. He finally wore me down and I agreed to make the trip with him in July 2008. The plan was

| Ankh | Abu Naga | Van Sertima | Newton | Runoko |

I would meet him in Cairo a week before my next scheduled study tour, we would tour the Western Desert over four days, spend two days in Luxor and then fly to Cairo where we would meet our group and then do our traditional fifteen-day study tour.

The adventure began when I flew into Cairo and was met by Abu and our driver whose 4-wheel drive Toyota SUV was loaded with supplies and camping gear. We drove to a local market to pick up provisions for our meals, and then we hit the road. Our route took us through a barren wasteland with no cell phone access, fortunately Abu Naga brought a satellite phone in case we encountered any problems.

After driving a few hours, we stopped in the middle of nowhere. Abu Naga asked me to get out of the car and examine the terrain. I looked around. There were no trees, vegetation, buildings, vehicles or people. There were just rocks and sand as far as the eye could see. Abu Naga asked me to examine the rocks that were scattered across the desert floor. At first glance I saw nothing special about the rocks. Then I noticed that the top and bottom of each rock had a series of concentric circles on the surface. Then it hit me. This wasn't a rock, this was petrified wood, which means that this area was once a forest and had been submerged in water. After thousands of years, the waterlogged wood turned to stone, and here I was, holding pieces of geological history in my hand. I realized at that moment that this was not going to be an ordinary tour.

We visited The Black Desert, a region covered with black volcanic rocks made of dolerite. We drove through Crystal Mountain – an area littered with quartz crystals of various shapes and sizes. We stopped at a guest house and swam in an above ground pool which was fed by water from a hot spring. We stayed at the guest house overnight and set out early the next morning to continue our journey.

After driving all morning, we sought relief from the blazing mid-day sun at Dakhla Oasis – a plot of trees, grass, and vegetation surrounded by an ocean of sand. Abu Naga and I walked around the Oasis while our driver prepared lunch. We came across a skull that had been discarded in shrubbery. A short while later we happened upon a group of men sitting in the shade of palm trees eating lunch. Abu Naga exchanged greetings with the men. They spoke awhile more, then they invited us to have tea.

The men appeared non-threatening. They spoke in Arabic while I drank my tea and observed our surroundings. I wondered what the heck these men were doing in this isolated spot. A short while later, Abu Naga and I could smell the food our driver was preparing, we thanked our friends for the tea and said our farewells. While walking back to our campsite, I asked Abu Naga who those men were and what were they doing in this god forsaken place. He responded rather matter of factly, "they're probably tomb robbers looking for buried treasure." It suddenly dawned on me that the skull we spotted nearby was probably one of their recent discoveries. This area was probably filled with ancient temples, towns, and tombs buried in the sand. There was no security, and anyone was free to do "personal excavations" without any governmental oversight.

The highlight of my desert adventure occurred during the last night and final day as we visited the White Desert. We arrived at our last stop in the early evening just before sunset. While our driver prepared dinner, Abu Naga and I gathered our sleeping bags and prepared our campsite for the evening. After a hearty meal, we sat around the campfire talking before retiring for the evening,

Holding petrified rock

During the middle of the night, I was awakened by a rustling noise in the darkness. The noise stopped when I unzipped my sleeping bag. It began again when I laid back down. I sat up abruptly and looked in the direction of the noise and it stopped once again. I stayed still with flashlight in hand. When the rustling began again, I turned my flashlight in the direction of the noise and saw the light reflecting in the eyes of a white desert fox scaveng-

With Naga in Pool

ing through our discarded leftovers. The fox quickly finished his meal and disappeared into the darkness.

This nocturnal encounter with the fox had my adrenaline flowing and I was unable to go back to sleep. I stared into the darkness for a while then cast my gaze upwards, and what I saw left me breathless. I saw stars as far as the eye could see and it was then that I understood the meaning of the phrase "a blanket of stars in the sky." I saw the Milky Way stretching upwards from the horizon and across the heavens, then I suddenly realized that I was gazing upon the same stars that my African Ancestors gazed upon thousands and thousands of years ago. I felt a mind-numbing connection to nature and humanity and as I drifted off to sleep these thoughts flowed through my mind. I woke up before dawn and felt a calling to walk in the desert to watch the sunrise.

The White Desert is apt-ly named because the area is filled with mounds of white calcite that appear to float in the desert like icebergs float in the ocean. Some of these calcite mounds were twenty to thirty feet high. Some looked like huge boul-ders and others had been sculpted by the wind and sand into familiar looking

Skull in the White Desert

shapes. One looked like a rabbit, and another had the face of a smiling polar bear. I sat on a nondescript white mound and watched the sunrise. As the sun rose higher and higher I saw my shadow grow longer and longer. I felt an overwhelming sense of serenity and I finally understood why my friend wanted me to make this trip. He wanted me to see these natural and manmade wonders. When I returned to the campsite, Naga asked me if I had seen the rabbit and the polar bear. I smiled, and he nodded as if to say, "Mission accomplished."

After breakfast we packed our gear and drove through the White Desert. Abu Naga pointed out other interesting shapes as we drove past the rabbit and polar bear. He pointed out two distinctly shaped mounds of white stone. He showed me a mushroom–which looked more like a mushroom cloud, and a whale. The rock he identified as the whale was about the size of a small school bus and looked nothing like a whale. I said, "that's not a whale," and he said it was. We went back and forth a few more times before Abu Naga told the driver to stop the car. Abu Naga pointed to a gaping hole in the white rock as we walked towards "the whale" and told me to look inside. I did and saw the impression of ribs embedded in the ceiling of this cavernous space. I was told that 37 million years ago this area was a sea teaming with prehistoric mammals that evolved into whales. When this creature died its flesh deteriorated and its ribs left an impression in the calcite that formed around its body.

Abu Naga told me he had taken European paleontologists on tours in the Western Desert and they found bones of dinosaurs in an area scientists call Wasi Hitan ("The Valley of the Whales"). I even found sharks teeth in the middle of the desert. My friend felt it was important to share this unique experience with me and I finally understood why.

Truck in White Desert

We left the White Desert and drove to Luxor. Abu Naga lived on the East Bank with his family. He arranged for me to stay in an apartment building he owned on the West Bank built on land his Nubian grandfather owned. It was here that I met Abu Naga's nephew who said that his uncle sent him to tell me about the work he was doing with the archeologist who had recently discovered the lost tombs of South Asasif.

I met Elena Pischikova the next day, and the rest, as they say, is history.

My tour of the Western Desert exposed me to unfamiliar territory, tombs, tomb raiders, archeological wonders and adventures that change my life. While mourning the loss of friends I was gifted with a unique opportunity to fund and participate in archeological excavations which allowed me honor Ancestors known and unknown.

Rabbit

Polar Bear

Mushroom

Whule

Karakhamun
Karabasken
Nesbanebdjed

Pour libation for your father and mother who rest in the Valley of the Dead. Amen-Re will witness your action and accept it.

Do not forget to do this even when you are away from home. For as you do for your parents, your children will do for you also.

–The Book of Ani

Recommended Resources

African Philosophy
The Pharaonic Period: 2780-330 BC
By Theophile Obenga
ISBN: 2-911928-08-3

Egypt
Child of Africa
Edited by Ivan Van Sertima
ISBN: 1-56000-792-3

Black Genesis
The Prehistoric Origins of Ancient Egypt
By Robert Bauval and Thomas Brophy
ISBN: 978-1-59143-114-5

SBA
The Reawakening of the African Mind
By Asa G. Hilliard, III
ISBN: 978-0-9655402-4-7

Nile Valley Civilization
A 10,000-Year History
By Charles S. Finch, III
ISBN: 978-0-9629444-4-4

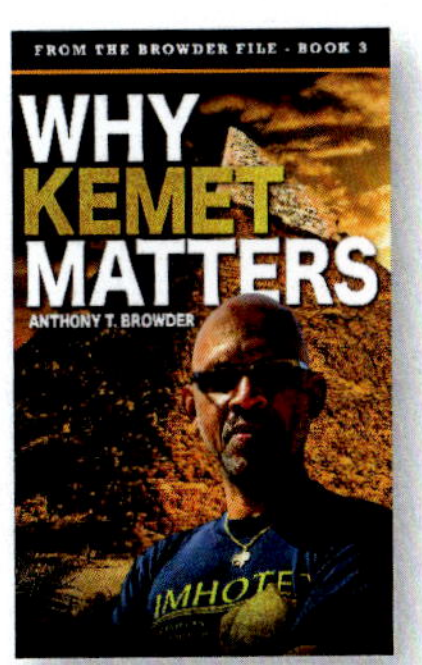

From the Browder File: Book 3
Why Kemet Matters
By Anthony T. Browder
ISBN: 0-924944-11-0

About The Author

Anthony T. Browder is an author, researcher and cultural historian. He has lectured extensively on topics pertaining to African and African American History and Culture.

Mr. Browder is the founder and director of the IKG Cultural Resource Center in Washington, D.C., and the ASA Restoration Project. He is the author of numerous publications which are currently used in classrooms around the world.

"Tony" describes himself as a chronicler of facts and information relative to the positive portrayal of the worldwide African experience.